REVOLT OF
THE CALL GIRLS

Jacqueline, with her independent ways, was doing the briskest business in all Paris. Madame Vannois, proprietor of one of the fanciest brothels, knew that meant trouble.

Madame Vannois' fallen angels confronted her.

"We want more money," demanded Suzanne.

"Jacqueline needs no such establishment as this," complained Roxanne, "and she has found herself a rich American, and *all* the money is hers."

"And," added Yvette, "she has a following of other gentlemen in very high places."

Madame Vannois pierced her girls with a glare. "Jacqueline will end in the gutter."

"No matter. We want more money."

"Perhaps. We shall see."

The girls left and Madame Vannois called her husband. "Imbecile," she addressed him, "we are in peril. You must concentrate on Jacqueline. *Jacqueline must be eliminated!*"

A Certain French Girl

by Nathaniel Tanchuck

An Original Gold Medal Book

GOLD MEDAL BOOKS

FAWCETT PUBLICATIONS, INC., GREENWICH, CONN.

MEMBER OF AMERICAN BOOK PUBLISHERS COUNCIL, INC.

A Certain
French Girl

I

"BUT JACQUELINE, what's the matter? Have you stopped loving me?"

"If I had, would I be going to Paris? Really, Pierre!"

"But a whole year!"

Jacqueline shrugged. "So?"

"So, she says!" Pierre rolled his eyes heavenward as though beseeching the angels to bear witness. "So why should Paul decide to go to Paris now? I'll tell you! So he could visit you! What will you do then? Throw him out?"

"Of course not!"

"Aha! I knew it! You and Paul . . . !"

"Don't be silly," she interrupted. "If he came to me in Paris, I would have to allow him in. He'd be a customer!"

"And I? If I came to you with a thousand francs? What then?"

"I couldn't accept your money."

"Why not? It's as good as Paul's!"

"Pierre, I could never look upon you as a customer! We're engaged! Besides, I couldn't allow you to spend your money like that! It would be like taking money from one pocket and putting it into another! So unprofitable!"

"Goddam the dowry!"

"Pierre!"

"I mean it!" he declared. "I don't want to be without a wife for a whole year! I'm a man. I need a woman. We'll go back and get married right now!"

She looked at him as if she could not believe her ears. Then, a soft love-brightness lit her face. She kissed him tenderly.

"Oh, what a beautiful sentiment! But we cannot do it."

"I should like to know why not?"

"Because the whole town will look down its nose at me.

7

I could not hold up my head, knowing that I was a charity case."

"A charity case?"

"Certainly, without a dowry, I would be nothing. I would be different from the other women. They would not accept me into their society—and I—well—*I* am a woman of pride. No! I must go on! And believe me, I will bring back a dowry greater than anybody ever had!"

She paused momentarily to emphasize her promise.

"I shall make you proud of me!"

Pierre nodded miserably. He shrugged.

"Anyhow, I wouldn't be able to go to Paris. I couldn't spare the fare, nor would I be able to spend a thousand francs."

"Of course not," she agreed.

And then, as she cuddled up to him in the back seat, satisfied that everything was again right between them, Old Thibault, who drove his clattering sedan-for-hire with the utmost attention to the road, suddenly shouted, "Station! And plenty of time to spare!"

They looked past Old Thibault.

Coming closer and closer was the little railroad station and the steel rails that seemed to join together at the horizon, pointing northward, directly to the wonderful city of Paris.

II

BEAUTIFUL AND lovely Paris!

Witty, light-hearted, warm-hearted! *La Ville de Lumière* in the spring night! Filled with *savoir faire* and *laisser-vivre* and fabulous *boulevardiers!*

A young girl seeking her future could come to no more exciting a center, so *française* in spirit!

Jacqueline stood in the railway station, cold and miserable. What a noise and a tempo! People bustled past her, talking and shouting. And such a vast ugliness was this building! If the architects who had designed this station had been imbued with a fiendish dislike of comfort, they could not have succeeded more admirably. Jacqueline shuddered inwardly. It was, indeed, a sight to dishearten the most veteran of travelers, and Jacqueline was a veteran of nothing. At least, not at this moment of her arrival. But despite this flicker of foreboding, her eyes absorbed the sight with the awe of a child first discovering the infinity of the rolling sea, with its impatient and noisy surf.

In one hand, Jacqueline clutched the plastic suitcase which enclosed all her worldly goods. The other hand clung to the letter directing her to her new home in this ancient hub of liberty, equality and fraternity. It had been given to her in the strictest confidence by Thérèse Tournay, who, almost a decade ago, had married Monsieur Tournay, the owner of the flour mill near Jacqueline's village. It was Thérèse's dowry, which she had brought back from Paris, that had initially purchased the mill. Jacqueline knew every word in the letter by heart.

To walk out and turn to the left until she reached the metro, was how she had to begin. There, she was to purchase a second class fare, so as to preserve her meager savings. At the Station de l' Opéra she was to descend from the underground train. She would see the Opéra commanding the place of its name. She was to walk to the right side of this glorious structure to Rue Lafayette, until she came to the business place of Madame Vannois, one door past the wine shop. She could not miss it because it was identified by elegant white script simply announcing, "Au Paradis". . . .

"Taxi, Mademoiselle?"

She felt a hand on her suitcase. Jacqueline cast her innocent hazel eyes at the taxicab driver, who stood wrapped in a wet and battered coat and a friendly smile. Tiny crinkles chicken-tracked the corners of his eyes, crisscrossing and disappearing in the ruddiness of his weatherworn cheeks. The way he gazed at her made her think of the farmer, Bouchard, back home, who was in the habit of pinching all the young girls whenever he could get close to them. She often wondered if Bouchard, who was a widower, pinched Yvonne, his daughter, who was as homely as an uncooked snail.

"It's raining," the taxi man's words came through to her, "and only a short step to my taxicab."

"I am taking the metro," Jacqueline's tones were polite, but practical, "besides, to Rue Lafayette I may not be able to afford the fare."

"Afford! Hah, Mademoiselle! In Paris one always manages to afford a taxi! To the metro in this rain will splatter your costly stockings, drip through your shoes, and take the shiny waves from your beautiful auburn tresses! Then think of the cost of replacement!"

Laughter spilled from her shapely lips, a happy laughter that was like a delightful bird-song. Men turned, smiling, and then their eyes lit up with the appreciation of a creature so utterly feminine, so much *la parisienne* despite the simplicity of her demure dress.

"So true, so true, taxi driver, lead on!"

And so, as admiring eyes followed the natural bounce of Jacqueline, the first principle of Jacqueline's ultimate philosophy of life was tucked away in a corner of her mind. To ride in taxis was a thing she would arrange always to afford.

Paris in the spring rain lay spread before her wet and shining. The windows of the taxi, with the film of water constantly dripping, muted the ancient buildings that rolled past. The only sound she heard was that of the Michellined wheels squishing along smooth pavement, and then squealing on cobbles. Her eyes fluttered from one side of the street to the other, slaking their curiosity on these venerable sights so new to her.

"Your first visit, eh?"

Jacqueline turned to the driver. He had swiveled his head around completely, grinning at her.

She gestured, "I do not want it to be my last! Attend the road!"

The driver disobeyed her command.

"There is nothing ahead of me so pleasing to look at," the driver beamed. "And I cannot talk to you with the back of my head."

"I suppose," she replied acidly, "you are able to see where we are going with the back of your head."

"Even without hands."

He lifted his hands from the steering wheel, and the car immediately slanted toward the nearest curbing. Jacqueline emitted a little screech. The driver quickly caught the wheel, twisted it, and came to a halt. Both sat momentarily silent. Unabashed, the driver turned to her.

"The rain must have warped the road."

He backed the auto slightly, and then proceeded at a more

leisurely pace. She said nothing. She shivered slightly and wrapped her cloth coat more tightly at her throat.

"Mademoiselle."

"Yes?"

"It is not so chilly when the sun is out."

"That's true of all France, not only Paris."

"Ah, but there are more places, and friendlier places in Paris to chase away the chill than anywhere else in the whole world."

"Have you been to places in the whole world?" She wondered why he was directing the conversation in this manner.

"No, but the whole world comes to Paris ... and talks to taxicab drivers." He swiveled his head, and his face was most apologetic.

"I regret I frightened you with my silly driving. I owe you more than a mere apology.... A glass of wine, perhaps?"

Jacqueline shook her head, "I have a destination."

"It will remain on Rue Lafayette," he insisted. "You may have coffee, instead, and—I should like you to see the one place the tourists have not discovered. You will like it. . . . "

"It is on our way?"

"Like the straight edge of a razor."

"Well," she reflected, "I wouldn't mind a coffee and a roll."

The taxi driver did not wait for the sentence to be completed. The small engine whirred, the car sped, down one street to another street, past row after row of shops, and an occasional church or two, finally entering a narrow street leading to the edge of the River Seine. The taxi halted in front of a small restaurant, whose glass windows glistened with moisture. Above was a listless sign hanging from a wrought-iron spear. It was a noble sign illustrated by the weatherbeaten symbol of knighthood—a medieval helmet on which was a plume ascendant. A closer examination of the plume revealed the full-blown charms of an extremely buxom nude, who stared out at the world with the eyes of a startled naiad. The name of the place, appropriately enough, was La Tête. Two taxis were parked nearby.

A strong odor of the sea struck the nostrils as one came to the entrance. It was no wonder. Just inside the doorway were several open barrels of mussels, prawns, oysters, and other delicacies of the deep. On sunny days, these barrels lined the street in front of the store, and cast their perfumery down as far as the old poplars which bordered the River Seine.

A giant of a man with a tattered coat sat close to the oyster barrel, guzzling the tender bivalves which he pried open with a knife. Opposite him was a red-eyed, red-nosed man who nervously struck at his proboscis with the back of a hand, which he used instead of a handkerchief. He was sipping a dark red wine. A bar and counter were on the far side of the café near the entrance to the kitchen. In one corner was a raised platform vaguely resembling a stage. An accordion hung listlessly at the rear. A piano and a bass fiddle were in use. They were not exactly being played in tune by the two men who were supposedly the current musical attraction of La Tête. First the man at the piano would run his hands over the keyboard, creating some sort of musical collection of notes. Then the bass fiddle tried to answer it, like a charade of string and percussion.

The sound bounced out to Jacqueline, moving her to snap her fingers softly and rhythmically, as she and the taxi man headed for a table. The proprietor, who was standing sour-visaged near his cash drawer, nodded.

"*B'jour*, Abelard."

The taxi driver raised two fingers.

"*Filtres.*" With a gesture of a worldly maître d'hôtel, Abelard gallantly offered a chair to Jacqueline.

She sat down and looked delightedly around. From the walls, the ceiling, pictures stared back at her. Some were yellow with age, most were flyspecked. The majority had been neatly clipped from movie magazines and swanky society periodicals. Jacqueline recognized one or two of the younger players of the cinema. But the most prominent were those of a decade before; some of them the days when nostrils flared, eyes rolled, and voices were mute. Beyond the fame of the pictured personages, there was a definite culinary affinity. Each photograph had been taken at a dinner or banquet. Here and there, attached to a photograph was a copy of the dinner that had been served on that occasion.

The big man and the red-nosed sniffler studied Jacqueline frankly. It was apparent they were enjoying their view. She looked at them and smiled brightly. They stood up and came over to her table.

"You brighten La Tête, Mademoiselle," the large one said,

his voice rumbling from within his cavernous girth. The sniffler nodded in emphatic agreement.

Abelard pointed at the two, "My friends, Tiny and Flic."

Jacqueline's brows arched briefly.

"Nicknames," said Abelard. "He is so huge we call him Tiny."

"I," said the smaller man, sniffling, "was once a traffic policeman, a *flic*. But I had to quit. Caught a cold and never could get rid of it."

Jacqueline held out her hand, "I am happy to meet you."

The two cups of *café filtre* were set down before them. The musicians stopped playing. They came to the table.

"Where did you find her?" admired the piano player.

"She is a passenger."

"With such passengers," Tiny rolled his eyes fervently, "I would be delighted to drive my taxi to the end of the world!"

Abelard preened with pleasure. The presence of Jacqueline had given him a new status. Already, however, she was sipping her coffee, enjoying its warmth. She glanced at Abelard.

"Drink up. I still must get to my destination before long."

Flic leaned forward, "Mademoiselle, outside is my taxi. I *own* it. Permit me to drive you, and there will be no charge!"

Abelard was indignant, "And my taxi, who owns that? I can take a friend without charging, also!"

Flic shrugged, "I suppose you will be able to explain the friendship to your penny-pinching partner?"

Abelard stood up. "I—I need explain to no one!" He turned to Jacqueline.

"Mademoiselle, you are right. It is time to go!"

She rose. He took her arm.

"A moment . . ." It was the piano player. He went to a table on which there were some flowers. He pulled the flowers from the vase which held them and came back.

"You are a lover of our music, I could see." He snapped a rhythmic finger, then bowed and handed her the flowers.

"Return, and you will hear music that even the birds can't match."

Abelard grumbled, "Birds! Cackling hens, he means."

Jacqueline smiled her thanks, and followed Abelard.

He helped her into the cab and went around to his seat. He started the motor.

"I like everybody, Monsieur Abelard."

Abelard grunted, "They're all right, but they're vultures. A man can't have a moment to himself with a pretty girl."

"But you seemed pleased to introduce me."

"To introduce, yes, but nothing else."

The remainder of the journey was uneventful. As he helped her out of the cab and picked up her valise, Abelard stared at the sign, startled.

Au Paradis! He turned and looked speculatively at Jacqueline.

Au Paradis!

Paradise, yes! But certainly not for so innocent an angel as Jacqueline. He stood there, the soft rain pelting his leather cap, dripping down his coat, wetting Jacqueline's suitcase. *Vraiment!* The young lady must be confused about the address. That was it!

"Mademoiselle," he cleared his throat diplomatically. "This place, ah-rum—you undoubtedly have made a mistake . . . it is—ah-rum—well, a confused address . . ."

Jacqueline looked him in the eye. She opened her handbag and took out the envelope and handed it to him.

"Here are the directions that I was to follow."

Abelard looked around for a place to put down the valise, then noting that it was dry at the doorway, stepped in out of the rain and set the bag down. He took out the sheet of paper and read it. His lips compressed as he carefully folded the paper and replaced it in the envelope. He extended it to Jacqueline, who returned it to her purse. The rain was beginning to spot her nylons. Her hair glistened like copper.

"Perhaps," Abelard insisted, "it is not that you have confused the address, but yourself. You see, this place is—ah —well-known to many of us. . . . It is—well, not a destination for an innocent . . ."

Jacqueline began to chuckle.

"You men! If I were to return to La Tête, you, the others, what would you wish to do with me? Serve me wine, allow me free taxis, hand me your money in tribute to my innocence? Would you admire me like an alabaster statue—or would you prefer me to melt with your desire?"

Abelard turned to pick up the valise, startled at Jacqueline's candor, embarrassed because she had come so close to the bone.

Jacqueline's voice was tenderly chiding.

"Ah, you men! I do not blame you, but then you should

not find blame if a girl is practical and wants to please herself as well as men, and not be free with her favors."

Abelard nodded. She was right.

"Mademoiselle, forgive me. It is true, I wanted to be a friend—a very close friend. I thought if I were able to whisper into your ear, that you would not object to what I wanted."

Jacqueline's laugh was clear and hearty.

"Come and see me here. You may whisper into my ear to your heart's content; but in any event, we can be friends.... Is it not so?"

She held out her hand. Abelard considered it briefly. Then, with a small chuckle, he took it and pumped it heartily.

"Of course we are friends! Woman to man or man to man, whichever you prefer."

"Now," said Jacqueline, in a practical tone, "what is the taxi fare?"

Abelard looked injured. "We are friends, Mademoiselle!"

"Friendship, that is one thing. Business that is another—besides, you have a partner and he is not my friend!"

Abelard beamed, "He will be, Mademoiselle, he will be. Even though he is a banker...."

He turned and pulled the bell. He and Jacqueline huddled in the doorway, out of the rain.

III

MADAME VANNOIS lolled in a huge circular bed, covered with a silken bedspread. A flowing Grecian style negligee and nightgown of sheer nylon draped her ample proportions. The upswept hair was copied from the classic Greek styles, carrying out the illusion of a hetaera of ancient Athens. At her side, a fluffy white cat rested under a caressing hand. On a small table next to her was a telephone and a huge box of bonbons. The color motif of bed and woman seemed to be entirely bright pink and royal purple. The drapes were drawn. A small lamp on a delicately carved desk cast a soft ray of illumination. Madame was popping chocolates into her mouth as though they were fuel to keep a furnace going. She would then clamp her mouth shut and make slurping noises as she sucked on the chocolates before biting them and swallowing. With a deftness that undoubtedly was arrived at through many years of practice, she spoke rapidly and commandingly to the man at the desk.

"I will not retire! Why should I? The figures you are mentioning prove that I am right, like always! Now, get on with your report!"

The man, nattily dressed, his thin hair plastered crosswise to cover a bald spot, shrugged. His eyes were red and watery, as if he had been spending too much time reading long columns of figures in badly lit corners. He reached a bony hand out to pick up a bottle of cognac.

"You are not to have a drink!" the woman's voice whipped at him. He withdrew his hand as though the bottle had suddenly turned into a rattlesnake. He turned pleadingly.

"But, my little rabbit, I have not had a drink for hours!"

"All right, Vannois, a thimbleful and that's all!"

Eagerly the man uncorked the bottle and without paying attention to the glass next to it, lifted the bottle to his mouth and gulped.

"I should be grateful," said the huge woman, as she popped a chocolate into her mouth, "that I have a husband who is only a drunkard and not a hop-head."

Vannois wiped his mouth with a handkerchief and then picked up a finger-smudged pince-nez and began to polish the lens. At that moment, there was a knock at the door.

The woman paused in the midst of biting into a cream-filled chocolate.

"The door, Vannois!"

The little man dropped the pince-nez. Springing up from his chair like a jack-in-the-box, he scurried to the door and opened it.

A blowsy woman, wearing a rumpled wrapper and a weary expression, glanced past him to Madame Vannois. The cigarette drooping from her lips bobbed up and down as she spoke.

"There's a kid downstairs. Says you're expecting her."

Madame Vannois looked sternly at the woman.

"A lovely picture you make for a visitor to see."

The slattern shrugged, "Next time I'll wear a Givenchy original to answer doorbells." She paused to take the cigarette from her lips, "What shall I tell the kid?"

"You tell her nothing. Just get back out of my sight."

Casually, the woman slouched out. Madame Vannois pursed her lips speculatively, then purred, "Vannois, how well is Suzanne doing?"

Vannois thought a moment, as if trying to remember.

"Answer me, Vannois!"

Vannois moved his shoulders Gallicly, and said, "She is not so much being asked for lately. But she brings in enough."

Madame Vannois sucked on a chocolate, thoughtfully.

"Ah, well, in that case I'll overlook her impertinence." She sat up straighter, fluffing out her pillow.

"Bring up our visitor."

Vannois nodded and left.

Madame Vannois arranged herself properly. She picked up an ornate hand mirror. A smudge of chocolate on the corner of her mouth she wiped away with a tissue. She studied her face carefully. In this light, with the carefully applied make-up, she did not show the lines of her age. The wisp of silk at her neck covered the sunken epidermis that no application of the beautician could cover. Satisfied that her appearance was impressive, she put down the mirror and arranged the cat so that it would appear that she was a study in casual royalty; or at least so Madame thought. The elegant box of chocolates would add a note of *éclat*, she knew. Actually, Madame Vannois sincerely believed that by receiving visitors, and other persons, in her bed chamber she was communicating to the world that somehow her blood-lines were piped into the past and glittering world of the Bourbon kings. She had impressed herself with this idea several years previously when she had seen and purchased a print of Louis XIV holding court while still in bed. Obviously, in such regal surroundings, Madame Vannois expected obedience and obeisance from all who were permitted an audience. She studied the chair to which she would wave. It was sufficiently far away so that her visitors could not judge how much of her face was makeup and how much was innately youthful. Also, the chair had been designed so that no matter how the visitor sat in it, he or she, as the case might be, would have to look up to Madame, both literally and figuratively. The fact that it was also a most uncomfortable chair in which to sit properly concerned Madame not at all.

Madame was aroused from her preparations by the harried tones of her husband's voice. She looked toward the doorway just as the little man skittered in.

"It's that girl, Jacqueline ... the one you were expecting ... but ..." His voice trailed.

"But what, Vannois?"

Before Vannois could reply, Abelard, clutching the valise in one hand and Jacqueline's arm with the other, entered. Vannois pointed at him as though he were a pariah.

"Him! He insists that he escort Mademoiselle to you. I told him that he could not invade your privacy and that ..."

"Knock it off!"

Vannois goggled at Abelard, who released Jacqueline's arm, put down her valise and cast cynical eyes toward Madame Vannois.

"What's this privacy stuff? You know me, Madame. Abelard the Taxi Man. Jacqueline's a dear personal friend. On my advice, she will talk terms with you *now*."

Madame Vannois looked haughtily at Abelard.

"My business is my business, and not for the ears of anyone not in my confidence—and *you* are not!"

Abelard nodded gravely. "That's the truth. I am not of your inner circle. But I know you well. All I want for Jacqueline is a fair shake."

Madame Vannois looked down her nose. "My establishment has been founded on the principle of equity. Now, if you will stop dripping rainwater all over my rug, and leave Mademoiselle to my arrangements, I will forget your impertinence."

Abelard started to retort. Jacqueline placed a hand lightly on his arm.

"Don't you worry, Abelard, I may be young and innocent, but I am not yet a fool."

Abelard stared at her briefly. "All right, but don't be sold a cat in a basket."

Vannois scurried to escort him out.

Madame studied the girl.

"Take off your coat."

Jacqueline complied with the order. She stood in her neat dress which revealed her shapeliness rather decorously.

"Turn around."

Jacqueline turned, showing the finer points of her curvaceousness.

Madame nodded in approval. She pointed to the chair. "Sit there."

Jacqueline walked to the chair and sat down. The chair

was tilted, and she almost fell against its back. She squirmed to settle in it comfortably. It was not possible. She looked at Madame Vannois, having to raise her head to meet the *grande dame's* eyes. She felt rather undignified.

"Now, then," Madame Vannois began, "what is it you've come to see me about?"

Jacqueline opened her purse and took out a letter.

"This letter of introduction should explain."

Madame took the letter and perused it carefully, despite the fact that she and Jacqueline were aware that its contents were known to both. However, it appeared that a set of niceties, as formal as a stately minuet, were expected, and both ladies did not want to upset this conformity of sociability and business. Madame would have been most delighted if she had been informed that such formality had long been the practice of the world of diplomacy, with the new arrival presenting credentials in the court of the reigning monarch. If approved, then the newcomer could become part of a new and glittering society.

"Excellent," said the queen of Au Paradis, and she put the letter to one side. She beamed at the girl.

"Jacqueline... if I may call you Jacqueline..."

Jacqueline nodded, "And what may I call you...?"

The woman's face assumed a haughtiness. "Madame Vannois... always *Madame* Vannois!"

Jacqueline nodded once.

"Now, then," said the queenly Madame, "you will live here. Vannois will show you your room. Clients will be arranged for you. There will be no need for you to concern yourself with that."

"I am only concerned with earning my dowry."

"Of course," Madame Vannois conceded, putting the cat, which was squirming, aside. The cat went to the foot of the bed and curled up comfortably.

"When you are not with a client, you will be expected downstairs in the bar."

"I am not an entertainer," Jacqueline pointed out.

"Your presence will be enough. Men spend more when they see pretty girls about."

"Do I get a commission if I am responsible for their spending?"

"Your commission is your board and room."

"Not a great incentive."

"No?" Madame raised her brows. "Do you realize how much you would be charged if I compelled you to pay cash?"

"I," said Jacqueline, "would prefer paying for what I had to pay, and using my time for greater profits for myself."

Madame sat up straighter, her lips thin.

"I have been in this establishment twenty—er—I mean ten years, and have arranged a set manner in which it is run. You may exceed a certain quota of drinks sold, and gain a small profit, but nothing more. Is that clear?"

Jacqueline shrugged. She squirmed in her chair, then moved to its edge and sat upright. Her eyes were more on a level with Madame's. The lady seemed a trifle disconcerted.

"You may stand up."

Jacqueline stood up. Her prospective employer studied her, pursing her lips.

"Fresh. Very fresh. You have the air of inexperience."

Madame stood up, slipped her veined feet into a pair of gaudy mules and walked around the young girl as though she were examining a mannequin.

"You will tell Vannois to arrange your clothing to show more of yourself."

She circled again, touched Jacqueline's hair.

"The color is good. It will not have to be dyed." Now she leaned forward and caressed and compressed the girl's dewy skin with expert fingers.

"The texture should prove exciting."

Jacqueline's eyes began to spark, her temper beginning to heat. She had not expected to be studied and judged like a cow.

"Madame Vannois, perhaps you would care to inspect my teeth!"

She curled her lips back to reveal sound and shapely oral formations.

Madame Vannois looked at her teeth, ignoring the evident hot tone which Jacqueline had used.

"Ah, you country girls! So strong!"

She stepped back now, to view the whole girl.

"Umm," she considered, "a certain group of businessmen, minor officials, should be dazzled by you. They'll pay well. Perhaps a thousand at a first introduction."

Jacqueline seemed impressed.

Madame Vannois turned, her negligee swirling. She reached for her bonbons and popped one into her mouth, and gestured that Jacqueline could help herself. Jacqueline took one and bit it daintily.

The older woman's voice had a gurgling sound as she sucked, swallowed, and spoke, all at the same time, or rather as close together as it was possible.

"With a new face and a new body, we can fool some of the men, perhaps. If they ask about other lovers you have had, be coy, embarrassed, perhaps shocked. . . ."

"Why?" Jacqueline's expression was quite candid.

Madame Vannois smiled wisely.

"I may arrange a greater price if they are led to believe you are a virgin."

"That shouldn't be difficult."

Madame Vannois grinned, "Smart girl."

Jacqueline shrugged, "Brains have nothing to do with it. I *am* a virgin."

The older woman's mouth opened like a codfish. Could her ears suddenly have turned traitor? She was positive that she had not heard correctly. Yet the words seemed to ring somewhere in her head. A girl, a girl standing in her establishment, directly in front of her, a real live girl had just said . . . ! But no, it could not be possible!

She eyed Jacqueline narrowly.

"You are a—*what?*"

"A virgin. . . ."

"You mean you have never permitted a man to . . ."

"Never."

"You swear?" Madame Vannois pinned Jacqueline with steely eyes, expecting her to falter.

"On my honor."

Madame Vannois buoyantly flung out her arms and pulled Jacqueline to her ample bosom and kissed her on both cheeks.

"Oh, you innocent! You sweet, sweet innocent!"

She released the puzzled girl and ran swiftly to the door and called out enthusiastically.

"Vannois! Vannois! Hurry! Quick!"

She stood in the doorway, glancing back at Jacqueline, smiling in a great and friendly fashion. Vannois came panting up the stairway, breathless and concerned. She overlooked the bottle of cognac he carried in a shaky hand.

"Gaze!" She pointed dramatically at Jacqueline.

Vannois blinked uncertainly.

"I gaze." His eyes flicked to Jacqueline and then back to his wife, puzzled.

"What do you think we can ask for her society?" She walked back, Vannois following, and both stopped to stare at Jacqueline, who was beginning to believe that she was on the fringe of the world of lunacy. Vannois glanced back shrewdly at his wife. Her attitude of excitement, almost that of a discoverer of a new world, or a recipient of news that her oil well was a gusher, came through to him. There was something of value in this girl that was not obvious to him, but which his wife sensed. He had a feeling that he should quote a good deal higher than ordinarily.

"Ah, I should consider that she seems to be out of the ordinary for a girl newly arrived to Paris."

He hesitated. Madame Vannois' enthusiasm overflowed with impatience.

"Bah!"

"Five thousand francs," he ventured.

"Bah! Bah! Twenty, thirty thousand, perhaps even an arrangement for only one or two clients! Vannois, behold! She is virgin!"

It was Vannois' turn to goggle. Automatically, he started to lift the cognac bottle to his lips. Swiftly, his wife snatched it from his hands. He recoiled nervously.

"But, but—my pet . . . !"

"Stop but-butting," she interjected, "and get some glasses." Vannois' mouth dropped open.

"Glasses!" The woman's imperious tones whipped at him.

Vannois jumped like a grasshopper. He bounded to a small, carved shelf, lined with glassware, selected three tumblers of good size and hurried back. Deftly, he cradled the glasses close to his chest, and freed one hand. He snatched back the bottle and filled two tumblers half full, and then filled the third one to the brim. He put the bottle down and without spilling a drop, handed the half-filled glasses to the women. Before they had a chance to even consider drinking, he began to gulp his drink.

"A moment, Vannois."

He stopped drinking, eyeing his wife with trepidation.

"This is an occasion," said Madame Vannois grandly. "We shall dedicate it with a toast."

Vannois sighed with relief. He stood to his full height, holding his tumbler high.

"What can I say on this great day? I think we'd better drink!"

He gulped, downing most of the contents of his glass.

Madame Vannois glared at him, then relented and smiled.

"Not precisely what I meant, but it has the sound of poetry."

Vannois, pleased, raised his glass again.

"I can make up rhymes out of my head all day. Here's another: There's a time to play and a time to pay, and . . . ah—and . . ."

Madame Vannois laughed, "The world has just lost a great artist."

She handed Vannois the cognac bottle, and gestured that he leave.

Vannois stared at her uncomprehendingly.

"You'll drink it on the sly, anyhow, with or without rhymes. Now, leave us alone."

Vannois turned and moved out slowly. At the door he stopped to utter a parting and face-saving remark to Jacqueline.

"Mademoiselle, it was an honor to meet a young lady of your virtue."

Mastering all his bantam dignity, he turned and strode out on his alcoholically propelled legs.

"Now, then," Madame Vannois turned to Jacqueline, "the arrangements have been settled. You will be the cream we will prepare and serve to a selected few."

She sipped her drink. Jacqueline put down her glass, appearing lost in thought.

The buxom woman eyed Jacqueline.

"If you have a problem, you may confide in me."

"It is only the problem of the arrangements," Jacqueline began. "I am uncertain what they are."

"Don't bother your pretty head with such trifles. Vannois handles all that. He handles the books of Au Paradis, you know. An excellent accountant."

"My pretty head is not concerned with the accounts of Au Paradis, Madame Vannois. It is concerned only with the year I spend in Paris, and how much I shall earn for my dowry." She paused a moment, then got to the heart of her problem. "It appears that because of my keeping myself to myself, I should not have to be here a year."

"Not be here a year? What nonsense is that?"

"Well, if you can obtain the fees you have mentioned, I should be able to earn a hundred thousand francs in no time. With such a sum, I shall be very rich."

"You would be, but I can see you know nothing of business. Naturally, the higher your fee, the higher your expenses. I shall permit you to entertain in this room, arrange exclusive modistes for you, as well as private tutors in manners, English . . ."

"I already like my manners and can speak English very understandably."

"Then," continued Madame Vannois, overlooking this interruption, "after all your expenses, and a few incidental commissions . . ."

"Incidental commissions?" Jacqueline's brows raised.

"Nothing for you to concern yourself with. . . ." Madame waved airily.

"Madame Vannois," Jacqueline's voice was flatly business-like, "you are a businesswoman, is that not so?"

The older woman nodded, rather pleased.

"So am I."

Madame Vannois stared at the girl, "You—a business-woman?"

"Yes, and I consider myself my entire establishment. Therefore, as an establishment, I should like to know precisely what I shall earn to keep myself on the profit side of the ledger. What I mean, Madame, I do not argue that we will share in what I earn, but what, I should like to know, clearly and precisely, will my share be?"

Madame Vannois was disconcerted. No one, but no one had ever spoken to her like this. Over the years, her girls accepted all her calculations without question. She raised a hand to her brow.

"Oh, my, I'm getting another of my headaches."

Jacqueline fumbled in her purse. "I believe I have some aspirin."

Madame Vannois glared at the young girl, who came up with a small bottle of aspirin and held them out with an innocent air. The woman pushed them aside.

"Because you are different from the others, I'll consider giving you a slightly improved percentage."

"And that is . . . ?"

"Fifteen per cent, after expenses."

Jacqueline's brow furrowed as she mentally tried to calculate what this would mean.

"It is very generous," Madame Vannois declared. "The going share is ten per cent."

Jacqueline stared at the woman indecisively.

"I—I should like to think this over before saying yes or no."

Madame Vannois shrugged. "I didn't send for you. You came of your own free will. In any event, while you are thinking, I'll have Vannois show you your room."

"No," came firmly from the young virgin, "I cannot stay here unless I know I shall remain. It would not be fair to you. I shall let you know tomorrow."

Before Madame could reply, Jacqueline headed for her valise. She picked it up and left. Madame Vannois shrieked at the top of her lungs.

"Vannois! Vannois! Where the hell are you! Vannois!"

In the deserted café of Au Paradis Vannois was opening another bottle of cognac, plastered to the gills, muttering to himself, "Purity is a surety... but cognac—should never lack..."

He never noticed Jacqueline letting herself out, virtually escaping from Au Paradis.

IV

"TAXI, MADEMOISELLE!"

Jacqueline still had one foot inside Au Paradis. Abelard was upon her valise, tugging it away from her. He had removed his damp coat.

"Oh, Abelard, I am glad to see you!"

"So is the sun, my pretty!" He nodded heavenward. "All Paris is shining because you have run from this—this!" He waved deprecatingly at Au Paradis.

He guided her to his waiting cab, plunked the valise inside, and opened the door, gallantly helping her in.

"I expected you wouldn't stay, so I waited."

"I was wondering how I would find my way back to La Tête."

Pleased, his face wreathed in a wide smile.

"I need your advice."

He eyed her sympathetically. "Papa Abelard is all ears. But wait, you can tell me what transpired while I drive."

He hopped behind the wheel, started the motor, and accelerated. Jacqueline leaned forward and reported all that had transpired. Abelard nodded thoughtfully at regular intervals.

At one point he exclaimed, "Aha! The bitch!" At another, he came to a decision, "This—this requires a great deal of thought, and more heads than just mine!" He took the shortest and most direct route to La Tête, unmindful of pedestrians and other sorts of traffic.

There were half a dozen taxicabs clustered in front of La Tête. The proprietor was leaning against a barrel of shrimp which had been rolled outside, sunning himself. Abelard deftly steered between two cabs and came to a halt. He cocked his head to one side and considered the other vehicles. He turned to Jacqueline who was getting out of the rear.

"We are fortunate. The shrewdest minds in Paris have already arrived."

Jacqueline studied the cabs briefly. "Those are their cabs?"

"After mine, the finest of the city."

Jacqueline glanced dubiously at the vehicles, all of which bore dented evidence of the Battle of the Boulevards. None of them was under three years of age. Abelard took her by the arm and wheeled her toward the entrance of the café.

He paused to speak to the proprietor, "I'm calling a conference, Solan."

The proprietor shrugged, "As you will—but one physical disturbance and I'll throw you out."

"Physical disturbance? Are you *fou?* Where in Paris will you find anyone so unphysical as me?"

Solan, the proprietor, appealed to Jacqueline, "He still owes me for three bottles of excellent wine crashed to the wall!"

"Vin ordinaire, that's all it was," Abelard protested, "and I've repaid you a thousandfold with taxi service!" He hastily strode away, pulling Jacqueline along with him.

Solan indignantly shouted after him, *"Vin ordinaire! Vin ordinaire!* I waste my good vintages and *haute cuisine* on louts!"

Abelard muttered, *"Haute cuisine,* ha! He dreams he's won the *cordon bleu."*

Jacqueline was too engrossed in her own problem to worry about Solan's dream.

Outside of one or two customers who were not of their circle, there were six cab drivers dressed in jackets, hats, and mufflers. Tiny wore his overcoat, which made him seem a formless monster. Flic sat close to Tiny, sniffling and wiping his nose. They were watching the other four playing *vingt-et-un* with a dog-eared pack of cards. Each man had a drink, wine or coffee, according to his whim and pocketbook. It was obvious that the dealer, a sallow-faced but innocent-appearing man of about thirty, was enjoying momentary prosperity.

"Alsace," said a disgusted player to the dealer, "if I didn't know better, I'd say you were dealing from the bottom."

Another player tossed in his hand in despair, "Or maybe even from the middle!"

Alsace pulled their money toward him, looking doleful. He was a man who always looked doleful, even when he was happy.

Tiny was the first to notice the return of Abelard and Jacqueline. He jumped up with a lightness that belied his bulk.

"My chair, Mademoiselle!" He offered it with a surprising grace.

"Sit down, Tiny," Abelard commanded. He turned to the others. "Suspend the cards."

Alsace began to protest. Abelard shut him up.

"Cards are for any time. *Our* good friend, Jacqueline, requires our help."

The men looked at Jacqueline with curiosity mingled with open admiration.

Alsace said gloomily, "And I was winning."

Abelard ignored him. He turned to introduce everyone.

"That long-face is Alsace. Says he's from there, but who knows."

Alsace nodded, unsmiling. Jacqueline held out her hand. He shook it. Abelard pointed to the others, each in turn.

"Henri the Egg."

Henri doffed his cap, revealing how he was named. His head, if he by chance would be asleep on the Sahara with it uncovered, would be a great enticement for a setting ostrich.

It was, indeed, a marvelous egg of a head, without a single hair upon it.

"Michel . . ."

Michel took off his cap. His hair was thick and black. He was a few years older than Jacqueline, strong-faced, and undoubtedly muscular of body and limb.

Jacqueline wondered, "No nickname?"

Abelard shrugged, "He has only newly joined us."

The last man was a roly-poly with twinkling eyes and a hearty chuckle. He stood up and bowed like a gentleman, kissing Jacqueline's fingertips. "Your servant, Mademoiselle. . . ."

Abelard grinned. "The Duke. . . ."

The Duke chuckled at Jacqueline's round-eyed expression. He spoke in cultured tones.

"I am only a pretender, Mademoiselle. The title is as worthless as that of any of the old Russians."

"You are Russian?" asked Jacqueline.

He shook his head, "Parisian, from the top of my head to the tip of my toes." He looked down at his girth. "If my toes are still there."

Jacqueline looked down at his toes. Gravely, she nodded. "They are there."

The Duke laughed. He chucked her under the chin. "A sense of humor! I like that! I like you!" He beamed. Abelard pounded the table.

"Enough of admiration! A conference is called!"

Immediately, each hitched up his chair closer around the table. Jacqueline turned expectant eyes toward Abelard. He pointed to a chair at a nearby table.

"Sit there, and you will be able to hear and speak when called upon."

Meekly, Jacqueline sat down as ordered.

"It is a question of Mademoiselle's establishing herself at Au Paradis."

As if each head were on a unit-controlled swivel, wide eyes turned to stare at Jacqueline.

"Attend me!" Abelard pounded on the table. The heads swiveled back.

"This is not an ordinary case. Our little friend requires to earn her dowry!"

"Ah," said the Duke, "a most admirable venture. It reminds

me of the classic case of Monna Vanna. In the play, she requires to save a life . . ."

"Spare us your plays!" Alsace declared in a monotone, "or we'll be here till midnight."

The Duke sighed. He glanced at Jacqueline.

"Culture has fled these walls."

Abelard shook his head, "Culture you can always catch at the Louvre. So let's everybody keep our remarks silent until I finish."

"Hear, hear!" Michel's voice was enthusiastic. The others frowned at him. He slumped back to become unnoticeable.

Abelard glanced back, "Solan! Wine for our dry throats!"

The proprietor reluctantly left his sunny spot and went to draw a carafe of wine.

"This dowry," Abelard continued, "must be collected within a year."

He paused to let this sink in.

"But we all know that bloodsucker, Madame Vannois. . . ." All did, as their grave expressions indicated.

"Expenses, commissions, and other charges leave little enough. Of that little, Madame Vannois agrees to pay only fifteen per cent."

Angry voices buzzed.

"Oh, that blackheart!"

"She's worse than my pawnbroker!"

"Quiet!" Abelard pounded on the table. They subsided. Solan clumped over to them with a carafe of wine and glasses. He plunked his cargo on the table. "How about something to eat?" Solan invited. "I've invented a delightful sauce. . . ." No one even looked at him. He sighed in defeat.

"Now," announced Abelard, "attend me carefully, for we are considering the problem of a friend."

He picked up the carafe and filled his glass. He turned and extended it to Jacqueline, who took it.

"*Merci.* . . ."

Abelard resumed his chairmanship.

"Of course, even at these terms, an attractive young lady will find more profit with Madame Vannois than as a housemaid or a waitress."

"Well," Flic wiped his hose, sniffled, and shook his head dubiously, "that depends on the circumstances. . . ."

Abelard smiled at Flic with a secret knowledge, "Certainly! The circumstance is this—" He leaned forward, savoring what he was about to utter. The others, sensing the great importance that was about to be imparted, hitched their chairs even closer in.

"Our Jacqueline has had no experience—with a man!"

All stared at Abelard, disbelief in their eyes.

Abelard nodded to emphasize his statement. Heads swiveled. Jacqueline sipped her wine. She moved uncomfortably as they stared. She put down her glass.

"What is this? Does the fact that I am unused make me a circus attraction? At one time or another, every female is untouched!"

"But at your age!" The Egg marveled.

"And to contemplate entering Au Paradis! That is a form of heresy!" The Duke's eyes rolled.

Abelard pounded the table. "Silence! Let us discuss the problem, nothing else!"

Michel broke in. "She could marry a wealthy man."

Jacqueline protested, "But I am already engaged!"

"And," declared Abelard, "*without* a dowry . . ."

Tiny, who had been silent all this while, rumbled, "In her condition she ought to establish herself, alone, without Madame Vannois."

All eyes fixed on the huge man.

Abelard agreed, "A suggestion worthy of being explored."

They all spoke at once. This one declared that she would need to share her income with no one. That one remarked that her efforts would not be abused, until finally Alsace made a typically gloomy observation.

"She would have the difficulty that applies to all new establishments. Au Paradis is already supplied with a steady clientele."

Briefly, this dash of cold water froze their enthusiasm. Abelard broke the silence with a sharp slap on the table.

"We are all idiots! *We* can select the clientele!"

The others gazed at Abelard, awaiting his wisdom.

"We are taxicab drivers."

All nodded.

"We know the streets of Paris as well as the palms of our hands?"

There was a murmur of agreement.

"And nobody knows the addresses of places like Au Paradis better than we, true?"

"Hey," cried Flic, forgetting to sniffle, "and we get first crack at most of the clients!"

"That's right," someone agreed. The Duke started to fill the wine glasses.

"And since we do," he continued to fill the glasses, "we can select only the most prosperous—noblemen, princes of wealth, and rich Americans."

The men snatched up their wine, "To Jacqueline. . . ."

They stood up to drink their toast. Jacqueline, in a small voice, thanked them.

"I appreciate your advice, my friends—but there are two small problems. First, how can you be certain that such glittering customers will appreciate me?"

"Appreciate you!" Abelard turned to the others, "How could they fail to appreciate her?" All looked at the girl as if she could not see her true value. Abelard told her.

"You are a virgin! They will demand to be of service to you!"

Jacqueline hesitated, for a moment dubious, then brightly she bobbed her head in agreement.

"In that, you have been confirmed by Madame Vannois."

Solan, standing on the fringe, to absorb the discussion, moved in to the table, to wipe it, but really to get a better view of Jacqueline.

"The second problem is what, Mademoiselle?" asked Henri the Egg.

"My purse. I have very little money. Not enough to rent a place to live."

"That is nothing!" Abelard waved airily. "Among us, we can advance your expense for one month, two months..."

Alsace came up with his pessimism. "Yeah, but where the hell can we find a suitable place for her?"

Where, indeed? The men looked from one to another.

"Around the corner."

It was Solan who spoke.

"Your apartment?" Michel inquired.

"The next building. The studio."

"You mean she'll share it with that unwashed artist, Vishevsky?"

Solan shook his head, "Exclusively hers. I kicked him out." He pointed to a corner of the café. "How long do you think I could afford to accept his lousy paintings instead of rent?"

Abelard pounded the flat of his hand on the table. "That

does it! She moves in right now!"

Solan held up a protesting hand. "Hold it! I'm not kicking out one no-cash customer, without getting cash in advance!"

The Duke stared down his nose at Solan, regardless of the fact that this action centered his gaze on the proprietor's Adam's apple.

"Cash in advance! Spoken like a true peasant! You should be ashamed of yourself, Solan. The mere fact that beauty such as this," he bowed to Jacqueline, "will adorn your rat-infested property, should be payment enough."

"Which we all guarantee," added Abelard, looking to the others for confirmation. They nodded. Alsace shrugged in agreement.

It was obvious that Solan didn't feel this guarantee had value. His eyes started to harden, but Jacqueline's innocent grace and beauty caused them to soften.

"All right, then. But remember, I allow this not so much because of your guarantee, but because I am impressed by Mademoiselle's innocence and honesty."

A huzzah ripped the wine-stale air of the café.

V

TO INSTALL Jacqueline in her new home was a simple matter. All that was needed was Jacqueline's presence and the depositing of her worldly goods, the valise and its contents. Ordinarily the appearance of the apartment would have dismayed the young lady. It was a mess. Heaped in one corner were paint-smeared scraps of newspaper and a number of tubes of colorful oils, already hardened from disuse and age. Scattered about were witnesses of the drinking in which its former tenant had engaged. Empty wine bottles, mingled with an occasional jug that had once contained brandy or vodka. In one corner was a bed with a bare and ancient mattress, whose scarred nudity evidently had never been covered by a sheet. A battered but solid hardwood table, with streaks and lumps of artist's paint, bore a single lamp, its shade made of a piece of old canvas decorated with an unintelligible impressionistic daub. But to Jacqueline, the huge window was a delight. The sun poured its brilliance and warmth through it.

Jacqueline gave a small cry of delight as she ran to the window and looked out. She was at the very top of this ancient building on the Rive Gauche. Through the window she could see the Ile de la Cité, with the Ile de St. Louis nearby. If she were to lean out and crane her pretty neck to one side, she had a view of the wonderful Pont Neuf.

"Oh, how beautiful!"

She turned a smiling visage to the taxi drivers who had accompanied her.

The Duke nodded in grinning agreement. "Yes, my girl. Before you lies all Paris, and nothing is more beautiful."

Alsace grimaced. "This is a rat's nest. The rat must be in there."

He went to a door and flung it open.

"Hey," he said in amazement, "a bathtub!"

If he had announced the Colossus of Rhodes, he could not have created a greater stir. The taxi men crowded into the open door.

"Magnificent!"

"Such grandeur!"

"As glorious a sight as any man could wish!"

Jacqueline, attracted by such praise, pushed her way through. She gasped.

"Impossible!"

They all were taken aback.

"It," Jacqueline pointed to the bathtub, "will have to go."

"But why? It probably is the life work of Vishevsky!"

"I wonder," said Henri the Egg wistfully, "who the model was. . . ."

The men sighed as they stared into the bathtub. In full reclining position, delicately brushed along the full length of the bathtub, was a softly curved nude, with the expression of one who is ready for love. Nothing, but nothing, was left to one's imagination about the painted lady's charms. Full-blown breasts seemed to float as on water, arms and legs were placed in comfortable and delightful (to the men, at least) position.

Abelard marveled, "No wonder Vishevsky never took a bath. It would be a waste of more enjoyable enterprise."

Jacqueline leaned over and scraped a fingernail on the

painting. Nothing came off. She turned to Abelard. "There must be some way this can be removed."

"Remove it? That would be a sacrilege."

The Duke silently examined the reclining bather from all angles, nodding and humming like an expert.

"It need not be removed," he announced.

"It must be! What will others think when they come in here?" Jacqueline was adamant.

"Do you care?" inquired Michel.

"The shape, the color of the hair, the face! Look closely, and then answer yourself, Michel!" Jacqueline pointed like an accusing angel into the bathtub.

"Le bon Dieu!" the expression was wrenched from Abelard's lips. He slowly clamped wide eyes on Jacqueline. The others pressed in more closely to study the reclining nude, then all moved as though hypnotized to study Jacqueline, who was nodding as though her judgment were being vindicated.

The Duke said most gravely, "The Russian must be a man of vision."

"More than that," rumbled Tiny, "a magician!"

"Are you certain," sniffled Flic, "that you have never been in Paris before?"

Jacqueline sniffed back at him. "I will not even dignify that with a reply."

"Uncanny resemblance," Abelard admitted. "You could have posed for that."

"I could have, but I didn't," Jacqueline's modesty was impressive. "To be seen like that—in a bathtub—is most indecent. I could not look into anyone's eyes with this in existence."

All nodded in agreement.

"The trouble is," the Duke volunteered, "it is affixed forever in the tub. I know of nothing that will remove it completely."

"I do," said Alsace, studying the tub closely at its connection.

They all waited for his solution.

"Replace it with another tub."

"Fah!" Abelard snorted, "Solan would never agree to buy another."

"He need not," the Duke's tone was filled with cleverness. "We shall."

A wondering expression filled everyone's face.

"You mean—you mean," Alsace asked warily, "that we purchase the new tub? Out of *our* own pockets?"

"I have a plan." The Duke bowed to Jacqueline, "This is a matter among us. I should prefer to confer without your presence."

Jacqueline cast hesitating eyes toward Abelard. He nodded, agreeing that her absence would be beneficial. Trustingly, Jacqueline went out of the bathroom. The men crowded around the Duke, who pushed the door shut.

The Duke's conspiratorially narrowed eyes surveyed the group. The men were jammed together against each other, the walls and the several instruments of cleanliness and sanitation. He whispered in spy-tones, "We sell this wonderful bathtub and buy a brand new one."

Alsace whispered back, "Optimist! A secondhand plumbing is never worth as much as a new one."

The Duke shook his head pityingly. "If this were merely a secondhand bathtub, yes—but it is more than that! It is a work of art!"

Abelard was dubious, his voice sotto. "That portion belongs to Vishevsky."

The Duke shook his head, "Not any more. Legally it is a portion of this studio, affixed as it is to the building." He paused to allow his knowledge of the law to sink in. "I know I can command a price excellent enough to purchase not only a bathtub, but a shower as well."

Flic protested, "Who needs a shower *and* a tub both!"

"Jacqueline does," the Duke whispered. "It is not only up-to-date, but impressive and so very chic."

Alsace snorted, "Why should we put in something that will belong to that bloodsucker Solan?"

Abelard was exasperated. "The hell with Solan! We do this for our good friend, Jacqueline!"

"Precisely," said the Duke.

"For Jacqueline," the Egg nodded.

"I'll get some tools," offered Michel.

"Then it is settled," decided the Duke. And all nodded.

With some twisting and turning, Abelard managed to turn the doorknob, and they strung out of the bathroom to stand before Jacqueline, who had, meanwhile, found a battered broom and begun to sweep up.

"Before morning," announced Abelard, "it is possible that the tub and that young lady in there may be replaced." Before she could reply, Michel scurried out. The others silently began to help Jacqueline clean up her new home.

Though they were not plumbers, the taxi men had little difficulty in disconnecting the artistic tub. Flic went hurrying to La Tête to make certain that Solan would not be in a position to interrupt their venture. Michel brought his cab around to transport the bathing vessel. Each of them grasped an edge of it and carried it down the stairs. Abelard discovered that it could be handled without his aid, so he returned to Jacqueline, to help her make herself more settled in.

"What," he pointed, "is that you are hanging up?"

"This," Jacqueline stated, "is a picture of Pierre."

Abelard walked over to her, to study the picture which she was hanging on the wall over the bed.

Pierre looked out with startled eyes and a self-conscious grin, which passed for a happy smile. It appeared to Abelard that the entire expression was one of a man viewing a sight that did not particularly delight him.

"He," pronounced Abelard, "could prove most disturbing."

"Disturbing?" Jacqueline was puzzled.

"Suppose," Abelard suggested, "I were a client. I look forward to complete happiness with you. I look at him. He looks at me. I go here not to be observed by his eyes." Abelard beckoned to Jacqueline to follow him as he walked to another portion of the room. He stopped and nodded toward the photograph. "Observe. His eyes follow." He took Jacqueline's arm and they walked to the opposite side of the room. Then both studied the photograph.

"Yes," she admitted gravely, "his eyes look at us."

They returned to the edge of the bed and contemplated the photograph. Suddenly, Abelard lowered himself to the bed. He glanced up from a supine position.

"Ah, like a vengeance he stares!"

He turned himself prone, and cast his eyes Pierre-ward. "Burrr!" he shivered. Then he stood up.

"Imagine! Alone with you and your fiancé is everywhere!" He reached up and took the photograph down. "My recommendation is that he should be hidden away somewhere."

Jacqueline took the photograph from him.

"No. I have no intention of hiding Pierre. He made this photograph especially for me to have something more than a mere thought of the future."

Carefully, she rehung the photograph, which continued to stare in its disturbing manner.

"But," she decided, "you have a point. Pierre can be like this when I am alone or merely having dinner with friends. However, when I am engaged in business...." She turned the photograph around on its wire, so that Pierre could see nothing but the wall, and others could observe nothing but the brownishness of the cardboard backing the photograph.

Abelard nodded in approval.

"Excellent. This way, neither Pierre nor your clients will be disturbed."

At that moment, the door opened, and Solan entered. Heaped in his arms were a long thin loaf of bread, a cheese and a sausage, and half a dozen unframed canvases.

"I found a few things I don't need at the café," he announced gruffly, as he walked to the table and dumped the food on it.

"Oh," Jacqueline's voice was grateful, "I shall pay you as soon as I can."

"Pay? Who said anything about pay? I'd only have to throw this junk out. Better it should be eaten."

Abelard took one of the paintings from him.

"Vishevsky," he shuddered. "This can't be eaten."

Solan sneered at him, "Maybe, maybe not. But it can be sold to some idiot, perhaps. Somebody who thinks it is art will be glad to pay good money for such originals."

"Then," said Abelard, "give it to a gallery or hang it outside along the riverbank where idiots go."

Solan shrugged. "I tried that once. No luck. But up here—who knows who might observe them and offer to buy." He cast shrewd eyes toward Jacqueline. "Besides, it will cover the bareness of the walls, and give an attitude of culture."

Jacqueline took one of the paintings. She closed one lid and studied it at arm's length with her open eye.

"Hmm! They are startling, but not too bad. Not too bad. You may hang them up, Solan."

With a triumphant grin, Solan took the painting from her and marched over to the nearest wall. From a pocket he took out several hooked screws and began to screw one into the wall. Abelard walked over to him and picked up the painting.

"I'll give you a hand," he said helpfully.

Solan merely continued to turn the screw into the plaster.

"An excellent idea to catch clients when they are in a most receptive mood."

Solan's eyes flitted suspiciously to the face of Abelard which was composed in unbelievable innocence.

"Under the spell of Jacqueline's innocence," Abelard continued, "how could any man refuse to purchase *anything?*"

Solan turned fully to Abelard, his lips compressed.

"So?"

"So," Abelard shrugged, "an art gallery makes a commission. These pictures on the wall that you are about to put up, make this apartment a sort of art gallery."

Solan shrugged in his turn, "The matter of a commission will be discussed when I see the rent—in cash."

Abelard's Gallic temper reddened his features.

"Camel! Vulture!"

Solan exploded, "Pig! You dare insult me in my own property!"

"Insult you, hyena! You can't be insulted! I—I—"

Their faces were close together, violence seemed imminent.

"M'sieurs!"

Jacqueline hurried forward and pushed in between them.

"What is this? A menagerie? You are both friends—good friends!"

Solan and Abelard stared at the girl, whose appeal struck them to silence.

She turned to Solan, "We have overlooked one thing." They stared at her quizzically. "Vishevsky. If one admires his pictures enough to buy them, then the artist has value."

"Bah!" snorted Abelard. "The only artist of value in case of a sale will be you."

Solan nodded in complete agreement.

"We still must consider Vishevsky. You Solan," she looked him straight in the eye, "will benefit by getting back the rent he owes you. I will reserve a small commission."

Abelard nodded in satisfaction, "That is all I was discussing."

"How small?" Solan was wary.

"Small enough to repay Vishevsky for his oils and canvas, and a little for the time he has put in."

"Bah!" said Abelard.

"Bah!" agreed Solan.

"The poor man," chided Jacqueline, "without a roof over his head, wherever he may be, penniless, without a friend ... who knows, even now he may be standing on a bridge ready to jump off."

"Good riddance!"

"Abelard!" Jacqueline was shocked. "It makes me very unhappy to think that you would refuse to help a friend in need."

"It's not his help you are asking for, *ma petite*," Solan righteously pointed out, "but mine. The money you are asking for belongs to me."

Jacqueline nodded, "Of course it does. That's what will make it so wonderful. A patron of the arts who has sympathy for the artist. Why, it will make him a hero! Besides," she added shrewdly, "besides, when I have a visitor, he will not only have these paintings to admire, he will require additional services—"

"Naturally," Solan leered.

Jacqueline shook her head, "I am not talking of myself. I am talking of you and La Tête!"

"Huh?" It was obvious from the way Solan frowned that she was as incomprehensible as someone speaking Neanderthal.

Abelard brightened, "Wines, food—your gastronomic sauces!"

Jacqueline smiled and nodded. Solan's eyes widened in anticipation, "Sauces! You will recommend my sauces!"

"Naturally." Jacqueline's shrug was most expressive.

Solan clasped his hands together in a fervency of joy.

"My sauces!" He glanced down at Vishevsky's work. "Foo! They will be as the artistry of Michelangelo compared to this!"

With renewed enthusiasm, he resumed driving in the screw.

Abelard turned to Jacqueline with renewed respect. He motioned to her that they leave Solan to his happiness. She grinned at him and followed him over to the bed. Abelard tweaked her cheek.

"Ah, you females! From the time you are old enough to

play with dolls, you already begin to learn how to twist men around your fingers."

Jacqueline frowned, "You think I did wrong?"

Abelard laughed, *"Ma petite,* you have the instinct to do everything right. Everything!"

He looked around, pleased. "Here, a man will be able to find all that is good in life, and obtain the culture of art at the same time." He lowered his voice, "But do not try to insist too much on Sauce Solan, for the sake of their stomachs."

He patted her cheek affectionately, "And remember, Pierre's face to the wall!"

He strode out of the apartment. Jacqueline looked to the photograph of Pierre, which still faced the wall. She contemplated it a moment, and then turned it face out.

Solan, who was ready to hang up the first work of Vishevsky noted this.

"Ah," he said, "a relative?"

Jacqueline smiled, "My future husband."

Solan nodded, "A fortunate man. A very fortunate man."

VI

"B'JOUR, VASSILY!"

The scholarly, full-bearded man twisted his mouth sourly. He bowed stiffly.

"M'sieur le Duc."

There was a subtle difference in the Duke's manner as he looked around the art gallery right off the Boulevard des Italiennes. His actions were assured and despite his shabby clothes, he was thoroughly at his ease. At the doorway, the other taxi drivers peered in, wondering. Henri whispered to Flic,

"A strange place to sell a bathtub."

"Shh!" ordered Flic. "There seems to be something more than meets the eye going on in there."

They watched, straining to hear what was being said. A strange tongue smote their ears.

The Duke spoke Russian.

"Vassily, I am giving you a great opportunity to discover a new artist. A struggling countryman of ours."

Vassily's sour expression deepened, "There hasn't been a good artist since the days of Nikolai."

"Not until Vishevsky."

"Vishevsky? Vishevsky?" Vassily shook his head, his beard waving slightly, "What is he, another communist bum?"

The Duke clutched at his chest, "That is like a knife in my heart, Vassily! That you, of all people, should accuse me of befriending a Red!"

"Bah!" Vassily's voice was contemptuous, "You, *M'sieu le Duc,* would befriend Lenin himself, if it brought you a few francs!"

The Duke straightened himself to his full height. That the day should come that an Ilyanov should speak thus to a Stepanov! "In the old days . . ."

"Yes, yes, I know!" Vassily hastened to cut him off. "You'd have me trampled by your Cossacks! All right, how much?"

The Duke relaxed. "That," said *Le Duc* magnanimously, "I shall leave to your discretion after you view this work of Vishevsky's."

He turned and waved to his co-workers. "All right, fellows, bring it in."

With alacrity, the taxi drivers hopped to the curb where Michel was guarding both his vehicle and bathtub. Huffing and puffing, they lifted it off the top of the cab and struggled with it into the art gallery.

Vassily had the expression of a long-bearded cod just dropped on land, flopping around for a drop of oxygen.

"A bathtub! A bathtub!" he screeched, his beard rippling as in a thunderstorm. "Take it out! I'm not a junkman!"

"Of course you're not," assured the Duke, "but before you chop yourself up like a herring, observe the artistry of this unusual painting."

He pushed Vassily close to the tub, so that he could see the glorious nude.

All closely observed the art dealer to see how he reacted. "Ah-hmm!"

Vassily cocked his head this way and then that. He pushed past the others, his eyes affixed to the nude, slowly circling the tub to view the nude from all vantage points.

"A Vishevsky, you say?" He spoke more to himself than to the Duke. The Duke nodded.

Vassily paused as he came back to stand next to the Duke and took a spectacle case from his pocket. He opened it and removed a pair of spectacles, then replaced the case in his pocket. He polished the glasses carefully with the white linen handkerchief that peeped out of a pocket. Most deliberately, he placed the glasses on his nose and ears and studied the nude.

"You're certain that he is our countryman."

Vehemently the Duke nodded, "On the honor of my family, I swear."

Vassily studied the nude again, unable to remove his eyes from her voluptuous contours.

"How much do you require, Excellency?" He beamed at the Duke.

"I have promised to replace this with a brand-new bath and shower, plus five thousand in cash."

"Two thousand." Vassily polished his glasses.

"A Stepanov never bargains with an Ilyanov!" The Duke appeared indignant.

Vassily sighed, "Three thousand and not a sou more."

"Make it four, you leech, and it's a deal!"

"All right, four," Vassily shrugged. "But on one condition." The Duke nodded. "Name it."

"Don't tell anyone that I bought this from you."

"Aha, you are a sly devil, Vassily! You're going to bathe in this yourself!"

Vassily glanced away, shy and embarrassed.

The Duke slapped him heartily on the back and winked. *"Chacun à son goût, eh!"*

Vassily's embarrassment deepened.

The Duke held out his hand, "Four thousand cash, and I'll send you the bill from the plumbing house."

Vassily pulled a fat wallet from his pocket and paid out the cash. The Duke thanked him, and headed out. Michel lingered as the others hastened after the Duke.

Michel ventured, "He's a real duke?"

Vassily eyed Michel blankly. Michel jerked a thumb toward the exit, "Him, the Duke. . . ."

Vassily nodded, "His father was a cousin three times removed from the Tsar." He added miserably, "Unfortunately for me, a cousin on my mother's side only twice removed."

Michel whistled in awe, "Holy sacred cow! And I thought

he was an ape who got his blue blood from studying poor but noble passengers!"

"Hah!" Vassily's face twisted sourly. "The only thing he has ever studied was how to diddle me out of money!"

Michel grinned, "That's a royal art in itself. Anyhow, you've got a helluva reason to bathe more than once a week here." He patted the tub.

Vassily's eyes guiltily sought the enticing form reclining on the enamel of the vessel.

"With her," Michel said cheerily, "a guy can have the cleanest affair in his life."

He sauntered out, wondering why the devil the bearded man had turned so shakily to glare at him as he left.

VII

THE ESTABLISHMENT of Jacqueline was ready for business. Already the new bathtub with its shower overhead had been ensconced in its majestic whiteness. The blemishes of the wall had been obliterated by the paintings of Vishevsky, which seemed less glaring than when first observed. In actuality, Jacqueline declared, their colors added a gaiety that the room required. The four thousand francs which the Duke had obtained, enabled her to purchase a new secondhand bed and other furnishings at the *Marché aux Puces,* under the sharp-eyed guidance of Abelard and the other taxi drivers. The men prided themselves in the great bargains they were able to close. Actually, however, it was the openly frank sweetness of Jacqueline which had melted the hearts of the hardheaded businessmen of Clignancourt.

Now that the studio flat was in a most comfortable condition, Jacqueline began to wonder how it would be to start in business. It was a matter to be discussed with Abelard and his council.

Abelard waved airily. "That," he declared, "is the affair of ourselves. You need not concern yourself with where the clients are. They will come."

Abelard and the others wondered how they could classify potential clients. To get the first one was a delicate matter. Flic shrugged. The simplest thing was to grab the bull by the horns. It would be easy to arouse any of their male passengers to a deep and quick interest in an obtainable virgin. But, unless they examined the passenger's social position, wealth, and willingness to part with a portion of his wealth, they would be failing in their mission.

Alsace demanded, "How does this examination proceed? You obtain a bank statement and a birth certificate from the man?"

"Nothing of the sort," sniffled Flic. "Ask him. Ask him right out, but first get a good look at his wallet." All spoke at once, until Abelard demanded silence.

"Flic," he decided, "has a thought. Leave the first client to me."

The others were delighted to permit this.

Solan, who, although not of the conference, felt that by the right of proprietorship he had a special privilege of voicing his opinion, offered a suggestion.

"A movie star would be ideal."

Abelard was disdainful. "The closest any of us ever got to a star of the cinema are your ancient pictures." He gestured casually to the numerous photographs around the place.

"Besides," said Michel, "there isn't one hanging around here who isn't a grandfather by now."

"Oh, yeah!" Solan bristled. "How about him?" He picked up a cinema magazine which was turned to a full page photograph of a handsome actor with his arm around a brittle but beautiful blonde.

The Duke stood up and took the magazine. He read the brief caption aloud.

" 'Will the Sweethearts of International Movieland Ever Set the Date?' "

"The story," advised Solan, "is on page thirteen."

Michel snorted, "Who needs to read the story. We all know it. Every day in the papers—Etienne and Maria—they are seen doing this, and they are seen doing that. Always together, and always in the same picture!"

"Aha!" Solan trumpeted victoriously. "But what is not in the papers is what very few know! Their latest super-grand spectacle, *Jolie, Jolie, Jolie, Jolie,* has a sneak preview this week, and only Etienne shall attend!"

He held out another magazine to prove his point.

Tiny glanced at the magazine, his voice booming, "Why all these *'Jolies'*? Wouldn't one be enough?"

Solan was disdainful. "That shows how much you know!

This is a spectacle of spectacles in the grandest of all aspects. A simple *'Jolie'* would not do justice to all the millions poured into it!"

"Hmmm!"

The gaze of all fixed on Abelard with expectancy. Abelard's "Hmmm!" was not an ordinary expletive. It was a note drawn from the depths of his diaphragm, expelled through the bellows of his lungs, then sonorously piped through his nostrils. It could only mean that Abelard had decided upon a plan of full-blown and swift detail. He would import it with consummate artistry, embroiling all of them in his scheme. It was a moment to be not only hopeful, but also extremely wary.

"We must arrange for Etienne Novembre's limousine to break down in a lonely place, and a taxi, with Jacqueline already a passenger, ready to come to his aid."

Henri the Egg's face darkened, "Why should his limousine suddenly break down?"

"Because," declared Abelard, "even a movie star's chauffeur cannot resist the treasury of France!"

He pulled a franc note from his pocket and waved it.

Michel snorted, "There's no real class in a movie star. Etienne Novembre! His real name's Ducrot. Used to drive a truck!"

Solan glared at Michel, "I don't care if he drove a stinking barge. I say my suggestion of a movie star . . . !"

"Quiet, Solan!" Alsace interrupted. "You're disturbing Abelard's train of thought!"

Solan's cheeks puffed out in anger. He hurled down his bar towel and went behind the bar. He took a sign from beneath it, and hung it on a hook screwed into the wall. It proclaimed: *Service Is Suspended For Credit. All Sales Cash.*

Flic reproached Alsace, "You and your big mouth! Now we'll have to pay him something on our accounts before we can wet our throats again!"

"All right, all right," Abelard pounded the table, and turned to Michel, "true, so he drove a truck; but what is wrong with a rendezvous with the screen's greatest lover?"

Michel's face shone earnestly, "He's only a guy as common as you and me who got lucky. No class! The type who figures it's a favor to give a piece of himself to any sweet young thing!"

Henri shook his egghead violently, "He tries putting one over on our Jacqueline, I'll punch his nose!"

Flic wiped his nose and muttered, "Me, too!"

Solan protested, "Stop puffing yourselves up into angry soufflés! Etienne Novembre, himself, hasn't been heard from!"

"Who has to hear from him!" Michel flung back. "That Casanova's an actor. A guy with a job, same as us. The only difference, he gets paid more. For a girl like Jacqueline, we require a prince—a prince of industry or of the blood!"

"I suppose," sneered Solan, still incensed because his brilliant suggestion was under attack, "you can shake such a noble personage out of your sleeve?"

"I don't have such a fine sleeve," Michel smirked, "but *he* has." He pointed at the Duke.

"I?" The Duke's brows curled like a question mark.

"I discovered," Michel announced, "from your friend of the art gallery that if you cut yourself, your blood will run blue. You are a real Duke, a man who must know where to find barons, counts, princes and people like that."

The Duke became the object of some surprise.

"You mean," Abelard was thoughtful, "you mean that he's a Duke—like somebody who—well—like the husband of the English queen?"

Michel nodded.

The Duke sighed.

All gazed at him with awe. The Duke shrugged in embarrassment.

"Come off it! I'm a taxi driver, no more, no less. That way I can eat, select an occasional bottle of good wine, and not have to bow and scrape for my dinner."

"Ah," said Solan, "no wonder you are the only one of this herd who has had a word of praise for my sauces!"

"Yeah," declared Alsace, "and I figured you were merely buttering him up to keep your credit going."

Abelard slapped the table with his fist, "What about it, Duke?"

The Duke merely shrugged. "Well, most of the noble persons I know are no better off than I am."

"That art dealer," Michel suggested, "he's a count or something, isn't he? And he has a prosperous business. And," he winked, "the way he looked at that nude in the bathtub, I'll bet he'll let loose of a pretty bundle for the real thing!"

The Duke shook his head, "No. Vassily and Jacqueline would be like oil and water. No affinity. But let me think. . . ."

He sat down. Solan ran back to the bar to fetch some wine. The Duke ignored the pitcher of *vin ordinaire* that the proprietor set before him.

"To think royally," the Duke announced, "I must drink royally—perhaps a bottle of Y'Quem."

"Y'Quem?" Solan's voice trembled.

Abelard slapped the table, hard, "You heard! When a royal duke drinks, hang the cost!"

"Hah! Next he'll be wanting Goldwasser with eighteen karat gold in it! The cost of that'll hang me!" Solan placed his hands at his throat and pretended to be choking.

The Duke stood up. He strolled slowly around the bistro, pausing here and there before a clipping on the wall. He stopped in front of one photograph of a pretentious banquet. He studied it with the air of a connoisseur and in a clear, quiet voice began to itemize the courses on the menu tacked beneath the eternal diners.

"Bifteck à la Buckingham avec sauce de Chef Ducrot."

Solan turned toward the Duke, like a compass needle that has discovered the pull of the north.

"Ducrot," the Duke smacked his lips. "Ah, I remember his sauce well. . . ." He studied the menu.

"Chef Rassen! Superb! There was a master to remember! His *poulet de Rassen!"*

"That was the first time it was ever served." Solan had forgotten everything in an ecstasy of drooling over the gastronomic arts. He shivered in delight as he walked over to stand next to the Duke.

"This was the dinner that made him famous!" He pointed reverently to the newspaper photo.

"Not the dinner, Solan," the Duke demurred, "but the guests—especially this one. . . ."

He pointed to an elegantly dressed man who occupied the seat of honor. Solan stared at the photograph and nodded, "Ah, Prince Igor Gertov! He was a man! Too bad he had to pass on! There was an eater! An epicure!"

"Such a one would make any chef famous, eh, Solan?" The Duke looked at him slyly. Solan nodded reverently.

"For him, Y'Quem, Goldwasser, anything would not be too good, right?"

"For him," Solan's eyes were veiled in a faraway introspection, and his voice rang with the fervency of the zealot, "I would spend a week making sauces, two days preparing a roast, and a day ransacking my cellars! Ah, but they do not exist like him any more!"

"That I can disprove."

Solan stared at the smiling Duke. His mouth dropped open in disbelief.

The Duke raised a hand and blew lightly on his fingernails, every inch the aristocrat prepared to put a commoner in his place. It was obvious to the others that the Duke was setting bait in front of Solan's nostrils. They waited impatiently for the trap to be sprung. Solan suddenly expelled a snorting breath.

"Hah! What are you, a resurrector of the dead? Everybody who can afford it is on a diet now. There are no more Prince Igors around!"

"Suppose," the Duke was weaving his web, "I brought a Prince Igor here. . . ."

"To bring such a one to La Tête would in itself be a triumph! I would offer music, drinks, choicest foods. . . ."

Alsace was flooded with disgust.

"You've got a crass tradesman's heart!"

Solan fired back, "Am I asking for money?"

"Bah! You're looking for the publicity, the fame!"

Solan appealed to the Duke, "You have an appreciation! You don't think I would do such a thing just to increase my business?"

Alsace laughed like a horse. Solan's face seemed like an overinflated red balloon.

"Out! Out!" he screamed.

"Hold it!" the command came regally from the Duke.

Sudden quiet smote La Tête.

"Solan," the Duke began a summation, "you would expect only the presence of Prince Igor?"

"But he's been dead for ten years!"

"Not dead, my dear chef, merely retired from the public eye!"

Solan's excitement mounted, "You're not lying?"

The Duke shook his head.

"That sign . . ." the Duke pointed regally, "it must come down."

Eagerly, Solan trotted over to the "no credit" sign and hauled it down.

"Now," said the Duke, "I see no reason why we should not arrange a surprise debut for *la petite* Jacqueline, regardless of Prince Igor's prolonged retirement."

The excited voices of the cab drivers drowned out the cry of the proprietor, demanding to know what assurance he could have that the Prince would attend La Tête.

Abelard waved airily, "Master of the kitchen, prepare your cooking fires and leave us to prepare the guests!"

At that very moment, without consulting her "board of advisers," Jacqueline was falling in love.

VIII

IT WAS a beautiful day. Through the studio apartment window, which she had polished a crystal cleanliness, the bright spring sun smiled.

The faint voice of Paris wafted to her like a stirring song.

She wanted to sing.

She wanted to dance.

A slight breeze ran its cool fingers through the crown of the poplars which lined the Seine below her window. An old woman pushed a *glace* wagon slowly past two children, who paused in kicking a ball to gaze longingly at the wagon. A man strolled by, breaking off a chunk of the elongated loaf of hard-crusted bread clamped under his arm. He chewed blissfully. He stopped his jaws working long enough to grin cheerily at the girl leaning out the window.

"A magnificent day, M'selle!"

Jacqueline smiled back at him. The man continued on. A trio of barges drifted with the tide of the ancient thoroughfare that was the Seine. The voices of the ball-playing children lifted to her. Impulsively, Jacqueline called out.

"*Glace!*"

The old woman paused. Her upturned face was carved with the erosion of many years. From the bend of her body, one could tell there was a great weariness in this ancient one. The sun, however, softened this weariness, shining in a face warmed by the gratitude of the old, for the loveliness of simply being alive.

"Give the children an ice cream," Jacqueline ordered, "I shall be right down with the money!"

The old woman nodded. Jacqueline picked up her purse, and like a small girl going on a delightful picnic, virtually danced out of the apartment.

Already the children were darting appreciative tongues at the ice cream they had been served. The younger, a short-cropped boy with a bruise on one knee, grinned at Jacqueline as she approached.

"You the lady who's buying?"

"Why not?" shrugged Jacqueline. "A day like this, a kid should have ice cream."

"Thanks for both of us," said the boy, and he gestured to his pal, "Let's play ball!"

And the two went hooting and licking and ball-kicking back to where there was more open ground.

Jacqueline smiled after them. The old woman sighed.

"They ain't got much manners nowadays. You want one for yourself?"

"Of course," Jacqueline smiled. "I'm as good as those kids."

She opened her purse and took out a portion of her meager funds and paid the old woman.

The ice cream was deliciously cool and so refreshing. She strolled along, savoring it, savoring the day, the life about her. How long she had been walking, or how far, she didn't know, nor did she care. Here she was, a simple country girl, the life and the fragrance of the most beautiful city in the world in her possession. People smiled at her, and she smiled back. The friendliest people in the world.

The riverbank turned slightly. She followed along, and suddenly she stopped. Her eyes widened with awe. There before her stood the most wonderful, the most beautiful thing she had ever seen. It glistened brilliantly in the sunlight. It was there on a barge that had been tied to the bank. It was a monstrous thing of metal, a thing of unparalleled strength. It was not simply born of metal and a drawing board. To her it was a thing alive, shouting, "Here I am, Jacqueline! I have been awaiting you!"

It was a thing hypnotic that clashed down upon her, obliterating for the moment all else in the world. She was drawn to it, eyes glazed with admiration. A giant of a thing!

All red and shining. A shining red more brilliant than the red of a setting sun, or any lipstick the magic of cosmetics could devise. There were gears, and a huge seat, and shining parts untouched by the red, but gleaming like highly polished bayonets.

"She's a beauty, ain't she!"

Jacqueline turned her bedazzled eyes to the man on the barge. Mutely, she nodded.

"You know anything about this kind of stuff?" The man hitched up his greasy dungarees. He was about thirty, and very dirty, despite all the water around the barge.

"It's—it's something for a farmer," Jacqueline ventured.

The man laughed, "I should say! It's the latest thing in farming equipment. A tractor of tractors. It turns the earth, plants, and even harvests, if you've got everything on it!"

Jacqueline nodded. Her eyes turned back to the machine in yearning.

"Is it yours?" she inquired.

"Are you kidding!" the bargeman boomed. "It would take me years to pay for this monster—even if I had use for it."

Jacqueline studied the machine, "I'm going to buy it!"

The bargeman goggled, "You out of your mind? You can't ride this down the Champs Elysées or anyplace else in Paris. It's got to be on the land—a farm."

"I know," she nodded. Then she looked up at the bargeman candidly, "You are delivering this to a farm?"

"Heck, no! It's going to the showroom. Over where they sell this kind of stuff."

"Would you mind," Jacqueline's voice was wistful, "writing down the address?"

"Mademoiselle," the bargeman said, "I don't mind at all, but I haven't a paper or a pencil."

"I have," said Mademoiselle, and she hopped onto the barge and took out the writing material from her purse. As the bargeman laboriously wrote out the required information, Jacqueline's fingers caressed the machine. The expression of her face revealed that she had lost her heart irrevocably. It was an expression that many men of her future would give much to see, but that they knew was not for them. Nor could they possibly ever compete with this giant of so much redness.

IX

IN THE cluttered apartment behind his art gallery, Vassily sat beside the Vishevsky bathtub blissfully contemplating the glorious nudity of its colorful occupant. Here was a woman! The contours of all the ancient goddesses, the seductive invitation of sex without the sordid smell of the body's juices! Nor the demand to utter tender inanities of love! Would he, like the ancient Greek sculptor, wish to bring her to life? He shuddered. Though he had the normal drives of a man for sex, he remembered, in disgust, his only contact with the flesh of a woman when he was merely seventeen. It had sickened him. He knew that he should have tried to overcome this revulsion, but instead, he kept himself free of womanly flesh. In a drawing room, at an exhibition, he never betrayed his inner dislike for such intimate contact, remaining cool, aloof, respectful. He had found, however, that he could fix his sexual appetite on an objet d'art—a nude in stone, or on canvas. But never, never had he seen one which moved him to his very loins as this bathtub!

He sat there devouring the nude's contours, imagining her arms about him, her sighs of delight. So engrossed was he that he failed to hear the jingling of the bell which announced someone's entrance into the gallery. It was the Duke.

The portly cabbie stared around, surprised to see the establishment unguarded. Then a small smile played on his face. He headed at once to the rear and up the quartet of steps that led to Vassily's apartment. He was not at all surprised to see his compatriot so fascinated by the nude. The Duke walked softly so as not to disturb Vassily's moment of bliss. After a moment, he placed his hand on Vassily's shoulder. Vassily jumped half out of his skin. He wheeled, his eyes distended, his nostrils flaring, his beard shaking. The Duke shook his head like a schoolmaster who has caught a small boy *in flagrante delicto*.

"When a man is in the midst of a love affair, Vassily, he should do it behind locked doors."

Vassily's momentary embarrassment expressed itself with indignation.

"How dare you invade my privacy!"

"Invade? The door to your establishment I found open to the public. But don't worry—your sex life is your own concern, and *our* secret . . . as it has been for years."

Vassily bit his bearded underlip with uncertainty.

"Ah, Vassily, Vassily," the Duke sighed. "You are not alone in this world with an eccentricity. I once knew a man who had mistresses by the dozen. He never touched them. All he asked is that they allow him to sleep with their underwear clutched to him. Then there was a well-known diplomat who wanted girls to parade only in high heels—and I have a book about sex that . . ."

"Never mind!" Vassily shuddered in disgust. "You are a taxi driver not a psychiatrist. You put filthy connotations on my admiration of art."

The Duke shrugged, "I don't have to be a psychiatrist to prefer women to bathtubs. Anyhow," his face was earnest, "I suppose I am partly to blame. It was I who introduced you to that young wanton in your virginity. And have I ever imparted to a soul your experience?"

Vassily sank back onto his seat. "Don't remind me," he said miserably.

The Duke put a commiserating hand on the bearded man's shoulder.

"One of these days, Vassily, put yourself in my hands, and maybe you'll be pleased to gaze upon the real thing instead of bathtubs and statues."

Vassily's eyes filled with distaste.

"You didn't come here to invite me to sleep with a woman?"

The Duke shook his head, "Vassily, I'm here to ask your help."

Vassily sneered, "How much this time?"

The Duke sighed, "Not a sou. . . ."

Vassily laughed derisively.

"I mean it," said his cousin. "This time I seek your help for someone else . . . *Igor!*"

Vassily goggled. He was very good at goggling. The Duke was always impressed by Vassily's resemblance to denizens of the deep. Hardly did he resemble the same one twice. This time Vassily looked very much like a catfish just caught and struggling for air. He was about to make such a remark, but thought better of it. There was no sense in offending Vassily. That bit about the sex fetishes was Machiavellian, for he had implanted in Vassily's mind that he must cooperate in order to maintain the Duke's desire to keep his secret. He knew that Vassily's mind was playing with this thought, and that Vassily would protest in aiding him to see Igor, but his protests would crumble when they ran into the wall of fear about the Duke's knowledge of his sex life. The Duke watched Vassily as he gulped air and began to breathe normally.

"After all," the Duke made his next move, "you are the only one of us that Igor sees without difficulty. It's his money that finances your gallery."

Vassily drew himself up straight, "I've repaid him many times over both in rare works of art and cash."

The Duke grinned, "Not like me. I've tapped him for thousands, until he doesn't like to look at me or my palm any more."

He made a gesture of a man asking for a handout. Vassily pushed his hand away impatiently.

"Igor needs help from you like I need three heads!"

"Maybe you could do with three heads—then you could gaze three times quicker at that naked thing." He indicated the nude in the bathtub. Vassily's eyes narrowed. His shoulders sagged.

"All right, blackmailer, how do you propose I arrange a meeting with the old man?"

"Simple. Pick out an object you know he'll like and tell him *I* am bringing it over."

Vassily burst into derisive laughter.

"You'll never get past the door! Alec still works for him, he'll take the object from you and boot you out!"

"All I want is the door to be opened to me. The rest I'll handle."

Vassily stood up, "Very well, I'll telephone Igor and tell him you're coming."

He led the way back into the gallery. He selected a small painting and handed it to the Duke. The Duke studied it a moment in admiration. Then, just before he left, he made a parting remark.

"That nude in the bathtub, Vassily, take my advice. Put her somewhere that the public can view her, and it'll bring you profit, not only in customers, but in a clearer outlook."

"Advice," sneered Vassily, "always advice! You drive your taxi and let me run my business!"

The Duke shrugged and left. Vassily turned and started back to his small apartment. Then, he stopped and pondered a moment. He lifted the telephone and placed a call.

"Martine? Can you come over? I require your opinion concerning a window display."

X

ALEC, PRINCE IGOR'S ancient manservant, had always stood as a bulwark between his master and the undesirable. Of all the undesirables, he considered the Duke the most scoundrelly. He never could understand the manipulations of the Duke in breaching the defenses so that Prince Igor would grant him an audience.

"If you'd asked me at his birth, I'd have approved the cutting of that rascal's throat," Alec rolled his eyes heavenward. "Even then, the blood of a Rasputin boiled in his veins."

"Whatever runs in his veins," the Prince replied, "pours out of his tongue in a torrent of delicious gossip. It helps revive my cold bones. Tell him I'll see him."

Alec shrugged. Before he had taken more than a couple of steps toward the door, the Duke was already in the study. In his hand, he carried an unwrapped oil painting. As Alec shut the door behind him, he heard the Duke speak softly.

"I brought you this canvas which I know you will appreciate; but it is nothing to the greater delights I came to offer you."

Alec hesitated outside the door, tempted to eavesdrop.

"Delights at my age? What can be delightful?" The Prince's muffled voice had uplifted eyebrows attached to it.

Alec almost bent down to peer through the keyhole. He conquered the impulse, however, and reluctantly strode away. Had he yielded to temptation, he would have been astonished to see the Duke, thoroughly at home, pouring himself a balloon of the rare Napoleon *fine* that the Prince treasured.

The Duke sniffed in appreciation, sipped and savored.

"Ah, it's like fourteen karat gold," he sipped again, "but if you want *eighteen* karat, a touch of Sauce Solan is much more golden!"

He glanced sidewise at the Prince. Despite his age, Igor still was a fine figure of a man. He stood almost six feet tall, straight as a ramrod. Though his hair had thinned, he kept it close-cropped so that he appeared to have no really balding spots. His aquiline nose was Roman in proportions. His eyes were bright, anticipatory. The true sign of his age was revealed by the tautly drawn, parchment-thin skin of his bony hands. At first glance, he appeared to be not a day over sixty. He would have preferred to be sixty or less. Those were the last days of his great appetites, in bed and at the table. Now, neither the body nor the stomach seemed to function as they once had.

That, the Duke knew, was the real tragedy of Igor's aging. This bit of retirement to a graceful old age was the propaganda Igor's ego had employed; but if the Duke could tempt him, it would only be through arousing the Prince's belief that his appetites could be restored.

The stomach first, then the other appetite, that was the Duke's plan. He knew how to arouse the fires that were dying: whether the fires would be hot enough to burn anything—ah! that was another horse at the well.

"Solan," the Duke kissed his fingers and rolled his eyes, "not merely the successor to Escoffier—he is Escoffier, reborn!"

Igor smacked his lips, "Ah, such a one is indeed rare. Where did you find him?"

"Through an even greater rarity—his inspiration!"

The Prince's eyes sparkled as they had not done for years.

"Come now, nothing can be more rare than another Escoffier."

"Come now, yourself, Highness. There are things stirring in Paris that you know nothing about, stuck away from living as you are in this dungeon!"

"Dungeon?"

The Prince looked around his familiar room, bright with the sunshine, tastefully decorated with antique treasures that were priceless.

"What else is it? A few rooms, a cleaning servant or two, a sip of this," he waved the balloon, "you dine simply, without company, and the only one you talk to is that gargoyle,

Alec." The Duke swallowed the last of the Napoleon in his glass. "Outside, Paris lives—and if your name is mentioned they wonder where you are buried!"

The Prince nodded, absorbing this new thought. He muttered "Greater than Escoffier—and a greater rarity." Tactfully, the Duke remained silent as the Prince lost himself in thought.

"What," asked the Prince, "what can be a greater rarity than a great chef?"

"I told you—his inspiration—Jacqueline!"

The Prince stared at the Duke as though he were an idiot.

"A woman? Imbecile, that is the most common commodity a man can obtain!"

"Ordinarily, yes . . . but this is the rarest thing in all of Paris, even in your day . . ." He paused and leaned forward, "A woman, a beautiful woman . . . a virgin!"

The Prince considered this a moment, then went over and poured himself a Napoleon. He drank it.

"A great chef, a virgin," his voice warmed. "It makes me fill with hot blood again, just to hear you speak."

The Duke bowed slightly. "Why just hear me speak, when both can be *yours?*"

The Prince studied his younger compatriot briefly.

"I realize that I will pay for their services—what will *you* want?"

The Duke was gracious. "To be restored to your affection."

The Prince grinned, "Aha, you scoundrel, there truly must be Rasputin blood in you."

He laughed heartily, inviting the Duke to fill his empty balloon glass.

XI

THERE HAD never been such a sight in La Tête. One moment Solan floated on a heavenly cloud. The next he was down to earth energetically combing and currying the entire establishment. Prince Igor, *the* Prince Igor, was to dine at La Tête!

This re-emergence of that noted gourmet into the world of gastronomics would be a triumph for Sauce Solan! The

Duke, remembering the bygone era of royal courtesies, insisted that Jacqueline be instructed in courtly manners. Jacqueline rebelled, saying that all this curtseying and fluttering of eyes was outmoded nonsense. Abelard sided with her. After all, this was not an affair of Romeo and Juliet. This was a matter of business. The Duke finally agreed. One look at their protégée, and Igor would be so overcome by her sufficiency of charms that stately manners would be superfluous.

With this settled, Jacqueline volunteered to help Solan scrub down the café. Fearing that they might be pressed into a labor gang by her, the taxi drivers spent more than the usual time driving their cabs. They figured it would take a day and a half, two at the most to polish up La Tête. And they were right. They drifted back as though there had been no unusual activity. The last to drift back was Michel. But he did not drift. He came dashing in to report that he had spotted Vannois slowly circling the street, staring about as though he were investigating a crime. Abelard shrugged. That little fellow was less harmful than a dead cockroach. He may have thought differently had he known precisely why Vannois was touring the street.

All her life, Madame Vannois had been motivated by an instinct for survival. Her devious maneuverings over the years had made Au Paradis an impregnable fortress against all onslaughts, including that unnaturally outlandish legislative trifle called the Marie Richard Law. It was because of this instinct that Madame had ordered her husband to keep an eye on Jacqueline and the denizens of La Tête.

She had an uneasy feeling that the status quo had been shaken by Jacqueline's impertinent refusal of her largesse. Suzanne and the other girls would never have had the gall to request Sundays off, had it not been for Jacqueline's rejection of service at Au Paradis.

Sundays off! Madame Vannois sniffed. The one day some of her wealthier clients were free to seek rest and comfort in the elegant beds of her establishment!

Au naturellement, she vented her wrath on Vannois, accusing him of being too much with the emptying of bottles and not enough with the iron hand of discipline. She forbade him a single drink. She locked all the liquor cabinets and hid the key in the small canyon of her huge breasts. Of course, the hiding place was utterly visible to Vannois. The filmy silk that covered Madame's proud mammaries scarcely dimmed their twin outlines, and the shadow of the chain and key dangling between the warm mounds merely whetted Vannois' thirst. Madame was too well advised of Vannois' appetites to mistake his yearning gaze for that of admiration of her jutting femininity. Deprivation of alcohol was a greater disaster to her husband than the closing of the road to sex. It was, therefore, a simple matter for her to compel Vannois to seek out Jacqueline and to convince her of her folly in refusing to accept the rule of Madame Vannois.

At first, Vannois could not comprehend why a lone, inexperienced *jeune fille* should be of such importance. Madame sighed. Vannois had no vision. A *jeune fille*, alone, was of no consequence; however, a *jeune fille* of such independent nature, allied with the cunning Abelard and his unscrupulous legion of taxicab drivers, could create a noise that would resound even in the *Chambre des Députés*. Its echoes might even call attention to Au Paradis, so that even the largesse Madame dispensed in certain high places would be insufficient to stem a sudden enforcement of the Marie Richard Law.

Vannois shuddered at the thought of being abruptly out of business. He could only agree when Madame uttered a final command. Should Jacqueline refuse to return to Au Paradis, then steps would be taken to suppress her free-lance activities once and for all.

The little man lost no time getting the highly polished Citroën that Madame permitted him to drive out of the garage behind Au Paradis. Still, as he approached La Tête, trepidation overcame him, and he kept driving around and around to gather his courage. At last, he realized that he must be brave in order to be able to retrieve the key to his beloved brandy from its fleshy cache. He parked a short distance away from La Tête, and walked toward the café with the air of a casual customer.

Unfortunately for Vannois, on his last turn around the block he had missed seeing Jacqueline leave La Tête to go to her apartment, the location of which he did not as yet know. His plan was simple. He would either see her in the café or obtain the information of her address.

Vannois blinked in surprise as he entered La Tête. It sparkled gaily in its cleanliness. Solan was behind the counter, carefully hand-lettering a large card. Vannois approached the proprietor. He cleared his throat.

"Arhhm!"

Solan glanced up at him.

"Pardon," Vannois said politely, "I seek a young lady, a friend of my wife, who I understand is also a friend of yours."

Solan stared at Vannois.

Vannois cleared his throat again. "She—she is only an innocent recently arrived from the country, and my wife and I—"

"Seek to make her not so innocent!"

The interruption shook Vannois like an earthquake. He glanced around like a startled rabbit.

Abelard stood in the doorway of the kitchen, holding a roll of tricolored bunting. Michel was right behind him with a hammer and a box of nails. Abelard approached the little man, who shrank back. To his relief, Abelard merely asked why he and his wife were concerned so suddenly for the welfare of Jacqueline.

Vannois shrugged. It was only natural. After all, they felt responsible for her coming to Paris, and since she was a poor girl, perhaps she would like someone to give her a railway ticket to return home.

"Ah," Abelard pressed a hand to his chest, "such kindness touches the heart, M'sieur. But you and your wife do not have to be concerned any longer. Our Jacqueline may not possess glass slippers, but already she has found a Prince."

Solan nodded pridefully, "Prince Igor Gertov!" He thrust the large card under Vannois' nose, "I, Chef Solan, have been selected to prepare the menu for a private banquet in *this* establishment!"

"Private?" Vannois' eyes darted from one to the other.

Abelard and Michel grinned, and Abelard waved the bunting. "A celebration to mark the debut of our young lady should be exclusive, *n'est-ce pas?* It is too bad I cannot invite you to see with your own eyes how well we direct her welfare."

Vannois murmured something about his delight at learning this, then immediately rushed out. A roar of laughter from the trio in the café drifted after him.

Michel's brow furrowed, "Think he'll come back?"

"That rabbit!" Abelard laughed. "I just put the cherry on the frappe of his fright!"

He handed the bunting to Michel and suggested that he start tacking it up to complete the beauty of La Tête.

XII

NEVER HAD there been such a hustle and bustle at La Tête. Prince Igor Gertov was about to arrive! Solan was in and out of his kitchen more times than a cuckoo in an overwound clock. A tricolor had been draped around the photograph which included the Prince. Another tricolor was spread behind the trio of musicians, who were playing softly, though aimlessly. Tables had been pulled together and covered by a white damask cloth to give the appearance of a formal banquet. On the side, another long, damask-covered table had been created. It was laden with serving dishes heaped with delicacies à la Solan, each seeming to be a baroque sculpture. The Duke stood before these dishes, eyes glittering with greedy delight. Tall, specially purchased candles lit the restaurant, romantically darkening the corners. Solan had, indeed, done himself proud. A huge sign on the door proclaimed: CLOSED TO THE PUBLIC. PRIVATE BANQUET RESERVED FOR PRINCE IGOR GERTOV.

In the small kitchen, eagerly awaiting a glimpse of the Prince, were all the other taxi drivers, minus Abelard, who was with Jacqueline in her apartment. Solan muttered as he stepped on Henri the Egg's foot.

"Move back, move back, all of you!"

Alsace lashed out, "Why do we have to be stuck in this hole? We ought to be out there at a table."

Flic nodded, "Sure, we're *regular* patrons."

Solan shrugged, "Do as you please. Only don't expect any service from me. I'm too busy."

"All right," Michel started to leave, "we'll help ourselves."

Tiny stopped him, "You think it'll be all right?"

"Didn't I just say so?"

"But," Tiny was dubious, "we agreed to remain out of sight. The Duke said it would disturb the Prince if we were sitting around."

"All I know," said Alsace, "at my age, being stuffed into a kitchen makes me feel like a sardine!"

He stalked out. The others followed. The Duke ran over to them.

"You're leaving?" he asked hopefully.

"With free drinks and food sitting around?" Alsace was incredulous. He tried to push past the Duke, who stood firm.

"My friends, we agreed. This was to be a dinner for two."

Michel laughed disdainfully, "I see places for more." He pointed to several of the smaller tables pushed into the corners. "And you, are you all dressed up to starve?"

"Friends, friends . . ." the Duke protested, tugging at his clean white collar.

Tiny rumbled, "Friends should be invited to sit down. To eat, drink, dance! Not be steamed in a smelly kitchen."

He bumped past the Duke. The others followed.

"All right," the Duke surrendered, "but no rough remarks this night!"

Henri the Egg grumbled. "What's he think we are? Ignoramuses?"

They sat down in a clump around one of the small tables. Michel looked at the musicians.

"Hey, birds, give with a happy song."

Without changing expression, the musicians upped their beat playing what they called their *le jazz hot.* Michel's foot tapped out the time. Then he stood up, and as the others applauded, began to dance, snapping his fingers. It was at that moment the door opened and Alec stood aside to allow Prince Gertov to enter. There was a deep frown of disapproval on Alec's face, but the Prince grinned from ear to ear.

"Hai!" His voice was jovial, "This is music to send the blood racing!"

The Duke laughed. Michel danced more wildly. Solan came running from his kitchen, bowing low, and gesturing toward the center table.

Alsace pounded the table, "Wine, Solan, wine! *This* is going to be a party!" The others pounded the table to welcome the old Prince who, in the candlelight, seemed much younger than his years. Solan guided him to his seat, picking up the hand-lettered menu he had so painstakingly created. The Duke pulled out the chair, as Alec snatched the menu from the chef. Igor nodded his thanks and sat down. Alec pored over the menu, his expression becoming more and more disapproving. Above the hubbub of music and voices, the Duke introduced Solan. Igor smiled pleasantly. He sat back, looking around, seemingly surprised that he was the only diner.

"An aperitif? A glass of wine?" the Duke invited.

"Neither!" Alec pushed past the Duke, dropping the menu on the table, "His Highness has a prescribed diet."

"For one evening, His Highness can live a little. Stop burying him before his time!"

The Duke turned to Igor, "This is an evening like the old days, eh?" He picked up the menu. "Hors d'oeuvres to whet the appetite..."

"À la Solan," that worthy interpolated.

The Duke nodded and continued, *"Sole Bretonne..."*

Solan bowed, "À la Solan..."

"Poule Parisienne avec..."

Igor brightened, *"That* is what I came for. Where is she?"

The Duke's brow furrowed, then he grinned, "Ah, your lady for the evening!" He bent lower and whispered, "She will be here soon. Meanwhile, examine the food."

Igor glanced over at the side table. "À la Solan, I presume?" Solan nodded emphatically. He ran to one side and returned quickly with a bottle of champagne for Igor's approval. Igor touched it, and nodded in satisfaction over its coolness. Then he peered closely at the label.

"Ah, vintage Krug! Very good!"

Solan popped the cork and filled Igor's glass. As though this were a signal, the taxi drivers hurried to the bar and took several bottles of champagne. Alsace shook his head in disapproval.

"Vin rouge, that's good enough for me!"

But when the bottles were opened, he was the first to fill his glass. Igor waved Alec's protests away. As he savored the heavenly champagne, he stood up and went over to the side table. Using his fingers, he delicately tasted first this dish, and then that. It was so obvious that he· approved of the food, that Solan began wriggling like a happy dog, wagging from head to tail.

"You *are* a discoverer!" he applauded the Duke. *"This* is *food!"*

"À la Solan," the Duke beamed.

"Eat! Eat!" Solan was ecstatic, as he gestured widely, encompassing everybody. In a matter of minutes the center table was crowded, everybody sitting around the Prince, leaving the seat next to him empty. Solan huffed and puffed as he kept opening champagne bottles, and saw to it that Igor's dish was kept heaped. Suddenly, Igor belched. He took a gulp of champagne, belched again, and stared at his empty chair.

"Stepanov!" he bellowed. "Where is my *Poule Parisienne?*"

The Duke stepped forward, "Any moment now."

As if these words were the magic formula, the door was opened by Abelard, escorting Jacqueline. She stepped inside, stopping to look around with a fawnlike grace. There was a moment of quiet, the quiet that allows a man to pay a tribute greater than any accolade.

Her auburn hair was swept up in a Grecian tie, enhancing the delicacy of her clear-skinned face. The simple dress, belted just beneath her young breasts, swept out gracefully over her hips, clinging to her limbs, revealing just enough to show the promise of her shapeliness.

"Ah!" the breath expelled from Igor's lips.

He stood up and bowed. Abelard nudged her. She curtseyed.

"Jacqueline!" Michel held up a glass. The others held up their glasses, and toasted her.

"Our Jacqueline!"

They rushed forward and surrounded her, escorting her to Igor, who quickly pulled out the chair next to him. She sat down. Igor's admiration was openly apparent. He sat down next to her.

"If," he declared, "the goddess of love herself had entered, I could not be more pleased!"

Jacqueline shrugged, "In candlelight, with a borrowed dress, and hours spent on a coiffure, even a simple girl from the country passes for a heavenly body. Especially," she picked up a glass of champagne, "especially if she is looked at through a number of glasses like this."

She downed the champagne, and looked around.

"You have met my friends?"

"All but that one," he inclined his head toward Abelard.

Abelard grinned at him, "Abelard." He held his hand out. The Prince grinned and shook his hand, "Gertov." Abelard waved at the musicians, "Hey, why're you birds silent?" They played. Everybody spoke at once.

"Let's dance," Michel jumped up and went over to Jacqueline.

"After I eat," she said practically. Tiny, who had several

heaped plates of food before him, pushed one of them across the table to her. Flic filled her glass with champagne.

Alec bent over the Prince and whispered to him. Igor glared at him.

"I feel fine!"

Alec shrugged. "All right, stuff yourself. Your place in the cemetery is already paid for." He stepped back, as though washing his hands of the whole affair.

Michel began to dance by himself. Abelard hitched an empty chair over to the Prince.

"This is the life, eh, Gertov."

Gertov nodded. Abelard indicated Jacqueline.

"A collector's item, don't you think?"

"And the price?" Igor said cannily.

Abelard shrugged. "That I will leave to your generosity."

"Clever dog!" Igor chuckled. "We change price to a gift—a lover's token, which usually makes a man pay through his heart rather than his pocket."

Abelard's chuckle revealed that they understood each other. He leaned across to Jacqueline.

"Chérie, soon as you finish eating, you should show the Prince your art gallery."

Jacqueline's nod was extremely ladylike. Igor seemed to be flustered.

"This—this art gallery, it is your place?"

Jacqueline nodded, "Just around the corner."

Igor thought for a moment, then he turned to Abelard.

"It is the gentleman's privilege to arrange an evening . . . with a lady. Because of my position, I would prefer showing the lady *my* art collection at *my* house."

Abelard frowned dubiously. Igor leaned his mouth closer to the taximan's ear, to utter a confidence.

"I'll be straight with you. At my age, unfamiliar surroundings may make me uncomfortable. That is a problem that won't exist in my own bed."

Abelard nodded sympathetically, "Then, it will be your art collection she'll see."

He started to fill their glasses with champagne, then slammed down the bottle and ran for the door, which had just been opened by Vannois.

"Hold it!" He held a hand against Vannois' chest. "Can't you read? This is a *private* party!"

Directly behind Vannois was a trio of fashionably dressed

girls, somewhat older than Jacqueline, but all with the unmistakable mark of the demimonde. Suzanne, perfumed and coiffured to the hilt, glared at Abelard and turned to Vannois.

"Say, what kind of a crummy deal is this?"

Abelard sneered, "There's nothing here for you. Run back to Au Paradis."

Vannois drew himself up to his full height and looked sternly into Abelard's chin.

"It is not proper for a young lady to make her debut with only males present. As a friend, therefore, I have brought these three."

Michel, who was staring tipsily at the newcomers, let out a cheer, "Dames! C'mon, let's dance!"

He lurched forward, but was blockaded by Abelard. Jacqueline, who was watching the entire thing with interest, called out, "Abelard, allow them in. The more the merrier!"

"Especially as they are girls!" Michel leered.

Abelard shrugged. He stepped aside. Solan whispered to the Duke, "I shouldn't have shown him my menu. He probably came back to smell out my recipes!"

The Duke reassured Solan, "All he's got a nose for is cognac." His eyes followed Vannois and his ladies as they headed toward the Prince. Abelard hurried to the Duke's side. His eyes glittered as he watched Vannois bow to Igor and introduce his companions.

"Suzanne."

"Yvette."

"Roxanne."

The Prince was charmed. Jacqueline leaned forward.

"Now we can have a party! Dance with them," she ordered the cab drivers.

Abelard slapped the Duke on the shoulder, "Aha! I've got it. Vannois is a spy. He's been sent to learn if the Prince is not a dream in my head. My next week's wages, he's got a new deal for Jacqueline."

The Duke shrugged. Abelard thought.

"First thing we've got to do is get the Prince and *his* lady on their way out of here."

"And the second?"

"Why," grinned Abelard, "those are very attractive companions Vannois has brought. And Jacqueline wants us to have a party. We've been supplied with everything—champagne, food, music . . ."

"And three charmers from Au Paradis, at no expense!" The Duke dug a knowing elbow into Abelard's ribs. He laughed. "Let's have a party that *is* a party!"

He went directly to Igor and bent over his ear. "These girls who've just come in, you don't want to get mixed up with them."

"I don't?" Igor's brows arched.

The Duke shook his head, "Not if you want to keep more than your nose clean. Ah—I suggest you leave with our little Jacqueline."

The Prince nodded, "Tell Alec to bring the car to the door." He glanced at the girls dancing with Michel and the others. Vannois was speaking soft and low to Jacqueline, who shook her head vigorously. Abelard pushed in between them.

"*Ma petite,*" he said clearly, "we'll be late for the opening of the art exhibit."

He virtually lifted her from the chair and headed out the door. Igor beckoned to Solan, who scurried over to him.

"Solan, your sauces are superb. Your wine selection excellent. I will sing your praises to the skies!"

Solan beamed and bowed. Pictures whirled in his head. *Maître* Solan, *cordon bleu,* three forks, or was it four forks? Proprietor of La Tête where only the rich dined!

He murmured his thanks, bowing and scraping, moving back, pushing into Vannois who was making an attempt to get to Jacqueline.

The Duke shoved a large drink into Vannois' hand.

"Have fun! Drink!"

Vannois sighed. He slumped into a chair and drank. He had done what he could for the moment. There'd be another time. Meanwhile, there was an ocean of liquor to slop down.

It wasn't long after Jacqueline had left on the first leg toward earning her dowry, that the candles began to sputter and die, and the music became lower and softer—and there was a mutter of deep voices mingled with the giggling of females who knew just what that muttering meant.

In a way, one could say that here was the establishment of an alliance between the serfs of Au Paradis and the rough knights of the not-so-shining taxicabs.

XIII

THE ANCIENT ormolu clock in the upstairs hallway began to strike. Alec, fitfully asleep in his room, stirred. The clock chimed away. Alec awoke with a start. Three o'clock! And the Prince had not yet rung for him! He slipped on his robe and bed slippers and hurried down to the Prince's room. He put his ear to the door. He frowned. He could hear Igor's muffled voice. It made no sense to him. Three o'clock, and the old fool was still awake! He certainly could not be making love to the young girl. Nor could he be discussing world politics. He started to lean his ear to the door once again, but discreetly turned away. After all, at the Prince's age, what could be more splendid than to pass away in the arms of such a Venus! As he shuffled back toward his bedroom, Alec deciphered the muttering he had heard. It made no sense.

"Ah, you have won my castle!"

Had Alec peered through the keyhole, it would have made sense, bizarre as it might be. Three o'clock in the morning—a man and a desirable young woman locked in the privacy of a bedroom—she in the sheerest of negligees, and he in pajamas, were playing an ancient game—chess!

Jacqueline held up a black rook, a yawn delicately stifled by her other hand. Igor pulled on his lower lip as he studied the chessboard between them. He hitched his chair more closely.

"Now," he said, "I better pay more attention to my moves, and less to teaching you the game."

"I haven't won the game yet?" Jacqueline wondered.

"No, my dear, not until you've captured my king."

"But," she protested in dismay, "I'll never learn to do that!"

Igor chuckled, "Well, for a beginner, you've done pretty well." He stood up. Jacqueline eyed the bed. Igor followed her glance and smiled.

"Have a good night's sleep." He started for the door.

"What's the matter?" she asked simply. "Don't you like me?"

He turned and stared at her, not understanding.

Jacqueline pouted. "You bring me here and dress me in this lovely silk. Then you play chess with me for hours. Now, you walk out. Is it because you find me offensive?"

"Offensive? You, child? Of course not. It is just that I know how ridiculous it would be for me to try to revive this old carcass of mine. It's had its day."

"Then," said Jacqueline, "I might as well go home."

"What! And make me seem even more ridiculous than I am! I was a fool to let that scamp, Stepanov, revive my interest in sex. But I am grateful that it turned out to be you."

He walked over to a small cabinet and opened it. He took out a jewel box and hefted it daintily. Then, he turned to Jacqueline and handed it to her.

"Stay, and this is yours."

She opened the box and gasped. An emerald pendant worth thousands blinked back at her.

"I'm an old man," Igor explained, "I have no heirs. I am a lonely old man, and you have made me less lonely. This evening will be our secret, eh?"

"But all we did was play chess."

"That's the secret." He chucked her under the chin. "We'll let the rest of the world believe that I am a chap of great virility. As a matter of further conviction, we'll make this a regular evening once a week."

Jacqueline laughed, "Truly, you are not an ordinary man."

"You, my little virgin, are not an ordinary demimonde. That emerald, you keep it or sell it, as you wish. For other evenings you spend with me, across the chessboard, there shall be additional payment. What do you say?"

"What can I say, except . . ."

"Except what?"

"May I go to sleep now?"

Igor laughed heartily. He kissed her brow.

"Sleep well, my love."

Jacqueline put on the pendant and went to bed.

Alec hurried past the ormolu carved clock. His head throbbed. His ancient joints felt as though they had been compressed into an egg carton. *Borzhe moi!* It was past ten o'clock in the morning, and the Prince had not called for breakfast! For all he knew, Igor might be dying! He suddenly skidded to a halt as he approached the Prince's bedroom. That roar of laughter! It was the laughter of a man heartily alive! And a woman's giggle! Alec moved slowly to the door. It was slightly ajar. His nose wrinkled like a sniffing rabbit's. The aroma was disturbing. Coffee! Mingled with the spicy delicacy of fried ham! He peered through the opening of the door. *Borzhe moi!* The young lady of the evening was still there. She and the prince were having breakfast, and enjoying it! Alec straightened his rumpled clothes, brushed back the wisp of his hair, and knocked on the door. Without awaiting an invitation, he entered.

The jolly faces of Igor and Jacqueline turned toward him. He winced inwardly. They had no right to appear so happy when he felt like a dying man. Jacqueline waved to him.

"Come, join us, Alec! I've made enough breakfast for an army!"

Alec eyed her warily. What was she trying to do? Point up his dereliction, upset his position in this household? Preparing breakfast for the Prince was one of his privileges. Here was this—this—! His mind went blank, he couldn't bring himself to think of such a common epithet. He started to stammer, "Your pardon, Mam'selle, but it isn't proper. . . ."

"Proper! Shmopper!" The Prince waved to a nearby chair. "If Milady wants to serve you breakfast, you eat breakfast!"

Unhappily, Alec obeyed. Jacqueline served him coffee, ham, and a hot brioche. It titillated his nostrils, stirred his gastric juices as they hadn't been stirred for an age. Despite his embarrassment, he soon found himself shoveling food into his maw, listening to his Prince and Jacqueline talking like a pair of happy lovers. Alec beamed at Jacqueline. Her ease, her naturalness melted whatever concern he felt. Besides, her youthful beauty made the entire morning bloom. His eye fell on the cleft of her bosom, so roseate under the silken negligee, and suddenly he leaned forward to peer more intensely. That emerald! His head whipped around, his brows virtually skidding to the top of his forehead, as he looked at the Prince in utter awe. Jacqueline laughed in delight. The Prince openly winked at her. They knew what was whirling about in Alec's mind, and they were not about to disabuse him.

"Oh," said Jacqueline lightly, "have I remembered to thank you for this gift?" She fingered the emerald.

"Not in so many words, *ma chérie*," the Prince beamed, "and I don't need words after what *you* gave *me!*"

Alec's mouth dropped wide open. Jacqueline popped a torn bit of brioche into it. He sat up straight, embarrassed.

"Eat," she said merrily. "You'll need your strength to take me home!"

"And," Igor's voice was almost youthful, "don't tarry! I plan to spend this afternoon shopping at Sulka's."

"Sulka's?" Alec gulped.

"I always have my haberdashery tailored at Sulka's, you know that!"

"Always? You haven't been there in ten years!"

"I haven't been alive for ten years, you mean. And now—today—I am once again a man!"

"And what a man!" Jacqueline toasted, lifting her cup of coffee.

Alec stood up carefully. "Will," he asked tentatively, "will Mademoiselle be our guest here permanently?"

"Rather," Igor waved airily, "part of our household, at least once a week."

Alec sighed in relief. "I—I had better arrange to drive Mam'selle." He turned with great dignity and left. Igor chuckled. He laughed. He roared. The tears rolled down his reddening cheeks.

"Hah!" he gasped. "Did you see his face! His conviction! Hah! Hah! We've got him convinced I'm rejuvenated! A lover who shall go down in history!"

Their laughter resounded through the hallway, chasing Alec along the corridor, causing him to move faster than had been his wont. Could it be possible, he wondered, to arrange for him to recapture his own potency? He straightened his back, his aches and pains forgotten, and marched toward his own room, feeling just a little bit gayer, a trifle more alive.

XIV

ALEC HANDED Jacqueline a sealed envelope before he ushered her into Igor's limousine. She opened it at once. It contained five thousand new francs and a brief note which read: "For a delightful breakfast, I kiss your hand. For your favoring me, the cash. The pendant please wear as a souvenir of our secret."

It was unsigned. Jacqueline carefully folded the note and the money into her purse, and turned to Alec.

"Would you mind making one stop before taking me home?"

"Of course not, Mam'selle."

Jacqueline smiled and quickly got into the car.

"Where is this stop?" Alec glanced at her.

Jacqueline, who had memorized the address of the Earth-King showroom given her by the bargeman, told him.

Alec's face remained composed. Since the evening before, nothing this amazing girl could do would amaze him. The affinity between a place of machinery and Jacqueline was no concern of his. He got behind the wheel of the limousine and deftly drove away.

Jacqueline relaxed in the luxury of its upholstered softness, not at all worried about her frock, which was more fashionable for the evening than for a Paris afternoon. Five thousand francs, new francs at that, ought to be sufficient to buy any tractor. Of course, she really didn't know its precise cost, but five thousand new francs! She was so absorbed in her own delight in her swift progress, that she was surprised at the quickness of arrival in front of the sales showroom of the Earth-King Machinery and Equipment Company of America, Incorporated; Paris and European Branch.

Alec opened the door for her and she stepped out of the car, pausing to study the huge poster in the window which proclaimed: EARTH-KING MOVES THE EARTH.

A man in an unwashed smock was dusting off two units of machinery. Two men, in identical dark suits, were at a desk in the rear, going through a pile of papers. Jacqueline's impression was of the small mustache that grew under the nose of one of them, like a displaced eyebrow. The other man had prominent lips through which huge, horselike teeth gleamed. The mustached one appeared to be the superior, for a huge white carnation was fastened to his lapel, like a badge of office. Behind the desk was a plywood partition with a door cut into it.

Jacqueline hesitated. The men appeared to be so busy that she was uncertain about disturbing them.

Disturb them she already had. The clicking of her heels had brought them to attention. The mechanic, mouth agape, his dirty smock twisted, seemed to be frozen in a position of eternal dusting. The two men at the desk looked up as though mesmerized. It was unbelievable that such beauty should be floating toward them.

Jacqueline came to a complete halt. Both men popped to their feet.

"May I serve you?" The Mustache was the first to speak.

Jacqueline looked around uncertainly.

"You are perhaps seeking an address?" Horselike-teeth gleamed through thick smiling lips.

"I—I saw a machine on a barge. I wish to buy it."

The men appeared to be puzzled. Jacqueline described the machine.

"Ahh," said Mustache, "our superior super tractor!" He cast an amused glance at Horseteeth.

"Are you certain you want to buy that particular machine?" Horseteeth grinned.

Jacqueline nodded firmly. Mustache and Horseteeth exchanged shrewd glances.

"One moment," said Mustache. He beckoned to his associates, and both stepped away for a conference.

"You think she is joking?" Mustache wondered.

"Gaze upon the vintage of her limousine and chauffeur," replied the other.

Mustache craned his neck. He was properly impressed by the limousine and Alec standing near it like an old retainer.

"And that single pendant?"

Mustache nodded. Horseteeth leaned forward more confidentially.

"Nobody but an heiress would wear so little jewelry, not care how she is dressed in the afternoon, and be unconcerned about the age of her car and chauffeur."

"But that monster of a machine! That white elephant . . . !"

"Shh! Don't belittle it! She wants it. Let's sell it. It'll remove the blot from our sales curve!"

Mustache was dubious; but he shrugged as if to say nothing ventured, nothing gained.

Both turned back to Jacqueline.

"To be perfectly honest," said Mustache, "it is the finest, most expensive machine we build. A great deal too much machine for a young lady like yourself."

Horseteeth dug his elbow into his associate's ribs, hissing, "So, one look at a customer, and you know!"

Jacqueline blurted, "My fiancé is a farmer! It is for him!"

"Ah," said Horseteeth, "a glorious wedding present!"

Jacqueline nodded, and looked around, "But you don't have it here now."

Mustache beamed, "It is in the back."

"I'd like to see it," Jacqueline requested.

Both men gestured toward a wide door in the rear. She went toward the door. They hastened to open it.

There it was! The magnificent machine that had captured her heart. Sunlight through a dusty window bounced off its crimson brilliance. Jacqueline went to the machine. She stood there drinking in its strength and beauty. She walked around it slowly, caressing it here and there.

The grace of her movement, the love that shone in her eyes dazzled the two salesmen. Mustache stepped forward to her, his face softening.

"Mam'selle, this machine, it was intended for sale to the government of Rumania."

"They did not like it?" Her eyes rounded.

"M'sieur Stanley, our vice-president who is now in London, didn't like giving it to them. He insisted we receive payment in cash."

"And," added Horseteeth, "before delivery. That is why we are so lucky to have it available."

Jacqueline's face fell, "Oh, but I don't want to take it now. I—I couldn't afford to pay out for it all at once."

The men felt very sad at the unhappiness of the girl.

"Oh," said Mustache in as comforting a manner as he could muster, "an individual could purchase any machine we have on the American plan."

"Really?" Jacqueline brightened. "What is the American plan?"

"An agreement by the buyer to make what is known as a down payment, and then make payments every month until the whole thing is paid."

"Then consider it sold!" Jacqueline happily pulled the five thousand francs from her purse and extended it to Mustache.

"Oh my," said Mustache desolately.

Horseteeth glanced at the money in a depressing manner. "How—how much do you have to have?"

"Well," said Horseteeth, "a down payment for a machine like this is well—ah—well . . ." He looked imploringly at the other man, "I—I never really figured it out. Have you?"

Mustache shook his head.

Jacqueline's eyes narrowed shrewdly, "Suppose I make a down payment on the down payment, wouldn't that do?"

The two men stared at her in a bewildered manner.

"This I will pay you to reserve the machine for myself," she waved the five thousand francs. "Then, I will come in each week and pay you more, until the down payment is paid, and then I will continue paying until the machine is mine—entirely mine!"

"But," protested Mustache, "that will take a long time. A very long time."

"I assure you," Jacqueline was thoroughly confident, "I will take possession of my machine before this year is over!"

"One moment," said Mustache. He took his aide by the arm and the two went into a whispered conference.

"It would be a feather in our cap to get rid of that monster," Mustache began.

The other nodded, "We can't go wrong. Right now, she's offering us more cash than the Rumanian government did."

"Besides," Mustache's voice was righteous, "I never did approve sending our finest machines behind the iron curtain!"

"And," concluded Horseteeth, "it will be a pleasure seeing such a well-formed decoration here each week."

Both men turned back to Jacqueline, beaming.

"Mam'selle, it is agreed. The machine is reserved for you. We will arrange the contract, and you may sign it when you return next week."

"You will come to my desk," Horseteeth grinned, "and give me your name and address, so that I may draw up this contract!"

"A moment."

Jacqueline whirled and gracefully ascended the machine. She sat down in the driver's seat, and grabbed the wheel.

"Ah," she said, her words filled with joy, "in all France, never has a bride given her husband such a dowry as *my* machine!"

XV

SPRING HAD become summer, and in sundry high places, diverse gentlemen of means and position had listened in amazement to Abelard, the Duke, and the other taxi drivers concerning the available companionship of a beautiful virgin. There was Binet, the famous designer of automobiles, LaClerc, of the government, just to mention a pair. Neither one of them had ever purchased an original oil painting in his life, but after an encounter with Jacqueline, they returned home, possessed of an original Vishevsky, and most enthusiastic about this undiscovered artist. Binet, in particular, had been so enchanted that had Jacqueline told him that the blank wall of her apartment was an undiscovered mural by Michelangelo, he would have demanded to purchase it. As he left his office that morning, he dismissed his driver, saying it was a wonderful day for a stroll. Then, as soon as his car drove away, he hurried to a taxi around the corner. He peered at the driver.

"You're not Abelard," he ventured, his nearsighted eyes squinting.

"No," rumbled Tiny, "Abelard is busy. He asked me to take you home."

"Home?" protested Binet. "I do not want to go home. I have an arrangement for *déjeuner* at La Tête."

"That's another thing," Tiny was extremely courteous, "your appointment for lunch will have to be for yourself, alone."

Binet's brows raised. "Myself, alone?"

Tiny nodded. Binet shrugged. "Ah, well, in that case, I will enjoy the sun, although it is a poor substitute for Jacqueline."

He handed Tiny a tip, and, as good as his word, walked. Binet felt he should be angry; but he chuckled instead. That girl, that Jacqueline! Could one be angry with the morning dew, or an evening rainbow? They were things of nature, of absolute naturalness. So like her sweet self. He would see her another time.

He turned the corner and came to an abrupt halt. A crowd

was gathered in front of an establishment of business. It was an orderly crowd, an admiring crowd. Murmurs of appreciation floated to Binet's ears. Binet was eaten by curiosity. He elbowed his way to the fore of the onlookers. For a moment, chagrin filled him. A bathtub! An old-fashioned bathtub at that! But wait! There was something painted inside the tub. He pressed his face against the glass window.

Gorgeous! Delightful! Venus and Aphrodite and—! He looked even closer. He had seen that face, or something resembling that face somewhere! Then he chuckled. It reminded him of Jacqueline, yet it was not she. In the corner a smear of a signature—Vish—was all he could read.

Vish? Vish? Vishevsky! He pushed to the entrance. The door was locked, yet he could see the bearded proprietor inside. He lifted his walking stick and tapped on the door. The bearded man came to the door and pointed to a sign, CLOSED.

Binet pointed to the bathtub and shouted, "I want to buy that!"

Vassily, for it was he, shook his head, "Not for sale!"

Binet was not to be put off so easily. "I," he declared, "am Binet, Louis Paul Binet!"

Vassily glared at him and waved him away. Binet considered this a moment, then took out his card case and extracted a card. He held it close to the door window. Vassily read it, then opened the door.

"Quickly, enter!"

Binet slid in. Vassily shut the door behind him. He bowed. "I regret, M'sieur, I did not know who you were."

"What's the idea shutting your shop in the middle of the morning?"

"Ever since I unveiled that painting, I have been bombarded with onlookers, browsers, admirers, who finger the nude, but have no desire or money to buy."

"How much is it?"

Vassily shrugged, "I have made no price. You, M'sieur, you admire it, yes?"

"It depends. What did you say the name of the artist is?"

"I didn't say." Vassily smelled gold. "Vishevsky, the great Russian artist."

"You don't say," Binet tried to hide his pleasure. "Vishevsky, hmm!" He cocked an appraising eye at Vassily, "You're Russian, aren't you?"

Vassily straightened, "But a citizen of France."

Binet laughed. "As one citizen to another, who's ever heard of Vishevsky?"

Vassily shrugged again. He was very good at shrugging. He nodded toward the crowd peering in.

"I could keep it here and charge admission. It's a greater attraction to the public than the Mona Lisa."

Binet considered the crowd a moment, and also shrugged. He could match shrug for shrug with Vassily.

"If I were not in the business of selling art," Vassily said truthfully, "I would install this bathtub in my own place."

"Hate to part with it, eh?"

Vassily nodded. Binet thought a moment, then brightened. "Take my card. Send this Vishevsky to me. He can do a painting in *my* bathtub. That way, I wouldn't be unhappy about depriving you of yours."

"But, but—" stammered Vassily.

Binet waved aside his "buts", "Keep the price reasonable, and I'll agree to a handsome commission for you."

Before Vassily could stop him, he turned and walked out, jauntily swinging his stick, and continuing his promenade. Vassily locked the door, and then began to think.

Louis Paul Binet had tried to pretend he had never heard of Vishevsky. The request to have his own bathtub painted undoubtedly was a ruse to meet the artist, so that he could deal directly with the painter. It seemed to Vassily that if one such as Binet was seeking Vishevsky, Vishevsky could possibly be one of the great undiscovered daubers that came to glory only after dying. Vassily muttered in his beard. If anyone were to discover greatness in Vishevsky, it was his prerogative, not some casual stroller's! He, Vassily, had brought Vishevsky to public attention, and he was entitled to handle all of Vishevsky's work on an exclusive basis. But first, he had to find Vishevsky without arousing suspicion that there might be profits. Ah, he had it! He'd tell the Duke that he had considered the artist's career, and that as one ex-Russian to another, it was his patriotic duty to raise Vishevsky from whatever gutter he called home. The shrill of the telephone at the rear of the gallery called Vassily from his thoughts. He hurried to answer it.

"Allo!"

Vassily stood up straighter, his face composing itself with deep respect. It was Prince Igor, sounding bright, and almost youthful.

"Vassily, I've discovered an artist!"

"You have, Your Highness?" Vassily was apprehensive.

"Not a very good artist," Igor's voice boomed, "but he's Russian."

"N-not V-V-Vishevsky?" Vassily was almost plaintive.

At the other end, Igor stared into the telephone and turned to Jacqueline sitting across from him at a chessboard. Against the wall was an unframed Vishevsky. Igor covered the mouthpiece and whispered,

"He's heard of him. That's promising." He returned to the telephone.

"He's a protégé of a very close friend. She has lost touch with him. I thought if anyone can find a lost artist, you can."

"What," asked Vassily warily, "does she want to find him for?"

"Business, strictly business."

"A competitor!" Vassily cried. "I cannot believe you, of all people would ask my help for a competitor!"

Igor chuckled, "Hardly a competitor, Vassily. Calm down. This young lady has sold some of Vishevsky's works and has a little fund she wants to turn over to him, but nobody seems to know anything about this canvas-dauber."

A gleam of shrewdness narrowed Vassily's eyes. "I suppose she has sold everything of Vishevsky's she owns?"

Igor shrugged and held out the phone to Jacqueline. "Here, you better talk to him before he gets me involved in business. I refuse to be involved in business."

Jacqueline smiled, "You ought to be. You'd become a real tycoon."

Igor laughed. He was always laughing these days. It was a joy to be treated as a contemporary by one so lush and lovely as this eternal "virgin." His thoughts shut his ears to the phone conversation. How he had laughed when Jacqueline reported to him the curiosity of Stepanov, whom she called the Duke, and those other taxi drivers about that first night. She had extolled the manly virtues of Igor to them, and the Duke refused to believe her. The taxi drivers were steadfast in their belief that Jacqueline could do nothing for a man the age of the Prince. She did not insist on proving otherwise, and agreed with them that she was still a virgin. What was it she had said?

"It would have made no difference, anyhow, regardless of age, even if you were fifty years younger, and we went to bed instead of playing chess. I remain a virgin. I shall always remain a virgin until I marry."

Igor's imagination flurried. There was something of logic in what she had said, but it was a fuzzy logic.

"Indeed," she affirmed, "with you I play chess. But there are those who seek more for their money. I submit, but only for business and not for love."

Igor nodded. He could see how her mind worked. The sex act, in itself, without love, could not deprive a girl of her virgin thoughts. In her mind, Jacqueline retained her maidenhead. That could be pierced only by the man she loved, after marriage. There was no arguing with such thinking. Actually, any man looking at her could not fail to be impressed by her utterly virginal expression.

The conclusion of the telephone conversation had been reached. Jacqueline hung up the phone and returned to her place and sat down.

"Your move," she indicated the board.

"No," said Igor, "it's yours."

She nodded, and picked up the white queen and knocked over the black bishop.

"Your king is in check."

Borzhe moi! So it was. Igor studied the situation. There had not been so much brilliance on her part as distraction on his. Then he began to chuckle. She looked at him as if expecting a trick.

"My king is not in check ... he is checkmated!" He leaned across to kiss her, upsetting the board, scattering the chessmen.

"You mean," her face was filled with incredulity, "I've won?"

Igor grinned, "Hands down!"

At that moment, there was a discreet knock at the door, and Alec entered.

"Mam'selle Jacqueline, Abelard's waiting in his taxi."

"So soon?" Igor protested.

Jacqueline smiled, and arose. "Remember, I told you I

couldn't stay too long. I have some business to attend to."

Igor nodded sadly. "It appears that you are becoming the tycoon."

"You don't understand. It is my machine. I must see it, and make another payment."

She left rather quickly.

"Hey!" Igor shouted. She stopped in the hallway and came back.

"What did you figure out with Vassily?"

"Oh, that! He's coming over to see me tonight and appraise the rest of the paintings. He says he is sure he'll locate Vishevsky for me very soon."

She raised a hand in graceful departure. Igor turned to Alec, "See her tonight," he marveled. "Imagine, Vassily is actually going to see a woman tonight!"

Alec smiled, "All I can say, Highness, is that I wish *I* were Vassily tonight."

Igor laughed, "Be yourself, Alec. Even at your age, you can handle the opposite sex better than Vassily!"

He laughed, kicking the chess pieces on the floor away from him.

XVI

VASSILY APPROACHED La Tête. He had left his tiny car a street away, desiring to reconnoiter before committing himself. An odor to please alley cats smote his nostrils. Delicately, he lifted his perfumed pocket handkerchief to his nose. He suspected an open sewer nearby, then he glanced with distaste at the open seafood barrels in front of the café. From within came the sounds of a piano.

"Vassily!"

A heavy hand slapped his back. He winced. He looked around and there was the Duke. The die was cast. He would not be able to retreat.

"I've just come from Jacqueline's apartment," the Duke smoothed back his freshly combed hair. "A delightfully refreshing bath!"

"Y-you bathe in her tub?"

The Duke shrugged, "She welcomes us all."

Vassily looked uncomfortable. "I—I am supposed to meet Mademoiselle here. Not . . ." He fluttered a finger upwards.

The Duke laughed, taking Vassily by the arm and propelling him into La Tête. Jacqueline and Abelard were seated at a table. Solan was talking to them.

"Solan," the Duke announced, "my cousin! A blood relative of Prince Igor!"

Solan smiled expansively, "Be seated! I, personally, shall introduce you to Sauce Solan! And a bottle of wine on the house!" He bowed and hurried to the kitchen.

The Duke grinned, "Praise his sauce to the heavens, and he'll feed us all, gratis!"

Vassily seemed not to care. His eyes were riveted on Jacqueline. He bowed awkwardly. "I—I am Count Vassily . . ."

"Oh," Jacqueline acknowledged, "the great connoisseur of art!"

Vassily preened. Ah, what a discerning young lady! He bent over her hand and kissed it. The Duke seemed surprised. He eyed Vassily thoughtfully. The art dealer was acting like a normal male. Could it be that Jacqueline had stirred a new condition in his cousin? She gestured to a chair. Vassily sat down, his eyes fastened on her face as she spoke.

"Even if Prince Igor had not told me about you, I can tell from your appearance of culture that if anyone can help me find Vishevsky, you could! Is it not so?"

Vassily nodded. To the Duke's further surprise, he took Jacqueline's hand again and gallantly declared, "Mademoiselle, for you I would find Tsar Nikolai, himself! But of course, there must be other paintings you possess?"

Jacqueline jumped up, "I'll show them to you!"

"Where?" Vassily dropped her hand.

"In my apartment."

Vassily turned a paling face to the Duke. The Duke shrugged, "It is for art."

"But . . . but . . ." Vassily was aghast, "we would be alone in her apartment. Discretion . . ."

Jacqueline was puzzled, "What has discretion to do with the admiration of art?"

Vassily had no ready answer.

"Go on," encouraged the Duke, "she won't bite you!"

"Of course not," Jacqueline murmured, "I am not yet a cannibal!" Without awaiting his agreement, Jacqueline tugged at Vassily's hand, and he followed her meekly.

The Duke chuckled, "Ahh! Our Jacqueline is truly an enchantress! I believe she can make Vassily appreciate more than still life!"

At that moment, Solan arrived with a platter of food. Before he could notice Vassily's absence, the Duke whisked the platter from his hand.

"Start counting your profits," the Duke hissed. "My cousin's going to buy all those awful paintings you hung up, and he'll want a good vintage when he comes back! From your cellar!"

Solan, the greed glittering in his eyes, hurried away to select a good bottle of wine. The Duke placed the platter before Abelard and sat down, stuffing food into his mouth.

"Dig in," he gurgled, "before Solan gathers his wits and wants us to pay for it."

Abelard, naturally, needed no further urging.

XVII

A few days after Jacqueline had made her payment on her machine, Steve Stanley, the go-getting, dynamic vice-president in charge of European sales for the Earth-King Corporation, arrived in Paris. He saw his baggage to the George V Hotel, and ordered a taxi to take him to the sales headquarters of his company.

The taxi driver repeated the destination with fervor.

"Earth-King Corporation!"

Steve Stanley recognized the knowledge in the driver's tone. He leaned forward in a friendly fashion.

"What's your name?"

"Abelard."

"Well, Abelard, you've heard of my company?"

Abelard nodded. His brain raced. "His" company! This American must certainly be a millionaire. A wonderful client for Jacqueline.

"A young lady I know does business with your company."

Steve became wary. He had been warned about these Paris taxi drivers. They baited a trap with a promise of beauty, and a guy woke up in an alley with his wallet gone, maybe even his throat slit.

"Yeah. That's nice."

He retreated to the back of his seat and lit a cigarette. Abelard knew enough to remain silent for the time being. He drew up in front of the showroom and let the American descend. Abelard waved aside the fare.

"I'll wait for you, M'sieur. Without additional charge."

Steve was about to insist on dismissing the cab, but shrugged and went into the showroom. One rule of his company was primary in the foreign market. Never, but never, offend the population. Remember you are a guest in their country. He wondered if the population included cab drivers. Another rule was, learn the language. He had studied French in school, tried blitzing it with Berlitz and Linguaphone, but all he could achieve was summed up by a French blonde in London. "You speak French with a Turkish accent. Steeef!" And she laughed and laughed. It was a sore spot with him. One day, he'd show everybody. He would pass for a real Parisian.

Horseteeth and Mustache were profuse in their greetings, which so embarrassed the handsome young American that he became gruff.

"All right, stop with the cheers! I'm staying in Paris to clean up some boo-boos!"

"Boo-boos?" Horseteeth was nonplussed. "They are a new type of Earth-King?"

"No," rasped the vice-president, "they're old types. Types we are stuck with, especially Model AGX 119!"

"But," protested his French representative, "we are not stuck with Model AGX 119!"

"We're not?" Steve sneered. "We had it sent here after sending it almost to the iron curtain. It bounced back with a heavy loss of shipping expenses, and it's still on our hands!"

"Not *our* hands," declared Mustache.

"It is sold!" announced Horseteeth.

"Sold?" Steve didn't believe them. "To what government?"

"It is not a government." Mustache was delighted to supply this information.

"It is a girl," Horseteeth chimed in.

"A what?" Steve couldn't believe they were not kidding him.

"A girl," Mustache confirmed.

"What sort of a girl?"

The two Frenchmen went into raptures.

"Charmante!"

"Heavenly!"

"Such an innocent!"

"Innocent!" Steve dripped sarcasm with every syllable. "Charming!" He paused and then shot out, "Let's see the sales contract!"

They showed him the sales contract. He read it slowly, the blood pounding in his head, his pulses vibrating like taut rubber bands. He put the contract down on the desk, and held himself still. A girl had bought the giant machine, all right; but on terms that would take her a quarter of a century to meet. From what he knew of the legality of contracts, this one bound the company hand and foot. The blasted white elephant would remain in this place without their being able to move it. It would remain there until this girl had it all paid off in the next century. And here he had arrived complete with plan and authority to dump the blasted thing off as part of the Point Four program, or was it Point Five? His head ached slightly. What he needed was a glass of hot buttered milk, and a cool, smooth bed! With unnatural calm he turned to the Frenchmen.

"I'd like to talk to this girl. Give me her address."

Mustache and Horseteeth were startled. They looked at each other. They had never obtained her address, had they? Suddenly, Horseteeth remembered.

"I remember! She gave us an address, a restaurant!"

"Yes, and we did not put it in the contract because we thought it was only temporary!"

"What," the words came from the American's clenched teeth, "restaurant?"

"Why—why—it's—oh, yes, La Tête!"

"La Tete? That means The Head, doesn't it?" The vice-president stared at them narrowly. The Frenchmen nodded.

"Brother!" Steve muttered. "I can just see myself informing our New York office that we have sold our ace piece of equipment to a French broad who lives in The Head!"

"And what," asked Mustache, "is so wrong with such an address?"

"Nothing—except, almost all of my superiors and *yours* served hitches in the United States Navy!"

He wheeled and virtually ran out, stopping when he saw Abelard grinning at him.

"All right!" Steve shouted. "So you knew I'd need a taxi!" He jumped in and slammed the door. "I want to go to The Head!"

"M'sieur?"

"The Head! The Head!" He slapped his head, "You know, in French. It's La—La . . ."

"Tête."

Abelard drove the taxicab away with great skill. After a moment Abelard ventured, "M'sieur Earth-King . . ."

Steve stared at the back of Abelard's neck.

"You talking to me?"

"*Oui*, M'sieur, I have not yet the habit of speech with myself."

Abelard had deliberately chosen to speak in French. He had winced when the American made an effort to converse in the most beautiful tongue man had ever devised. It had come to him that this American was not the sort he could interest in a young lady simply for the young lady's physical attributes. However, if he could lead this young man along a path which was bordered with the virtues of improvement— say, the promise of being able to speak like a true Parisian—it could possibly lead to a better life for him and Jacqueline. Abelard had quickly digested the fact of this American's position with the Earth-King company. He had seen how subservient the two French salesmen had been. He had heard enough to understand that the present state of agitation which possessed this powerful official of the Earth-King company had come about because of the method in which Jacqueline had made her purchase. Now, this American, he could hardly be more than a few years older then Jacqueline. Not only was he rich, he was handsome in a very manly way. Far more handsome than Pierre. Marriage, naturally, had not entered Abelard's mind; but he toyed with a notion that was even better than that for Jacqueline. An arrangement could be effected whereby this American would consider devoting his time and fortune to her, in exchange for which he would be able to obtain a good deal of devotion from Jacqueline. It would also make him forget to press the matter of the sales contract for the machine.

Abelard spoke swiftly in French. "You are going to remain in Paris long, or are you planning to leave soon?"

"Hey, you want me to understand," replied Steve in his abominable French, "speak slowly."

"Perhaps I better speak English," Abelard suggested.

"No, no. Speak French. I'm trying to improve my French. How'll I be able to do it by speaking English?"

"I'm afraid," Abelard spoke slowly and regretfully, "that you will never improve your language that way."

Steve bent over the top of the front seat, thoroughly interested.

"Why not? I've tried all the shortcuts. Living right here in Paris for the next few months, I ought to be able to pick up on my French."

"Living where? The George Cinq? Where you got into my taxi? That is a hotel full of Americans who want to live like Americans and say they are in Paris. What you should do is live like a Frenchman!"

Steve snorted, "In one of those crummy third-class hotels with one bath for everybody?"

"No, no. That is for tourists. You should make an arrangement to live like a resident. There is only one way to learn a foreign language. Find an appealing girl and live with her. You'll have to make yourself understood if you want anything—and she'll be only too happy to improve your tongue."

"I heard that's the best way," Steve nodded, "but where will I meet such a girl?"

"M'sieur, you are fortunate. I, Abelard, can introduce you to such a girl."

Steve eyed Abelard suspiciously. "I wouldn't be interested in the kind of female a taxi driver can introduce."

Abelard shrugged, "Only a suggestion, M'sieur." He turned his complete attention to driving. Steve was chagrined over the abrupt end of the conversation.

"You see," he stumbled in French, "a man in my position must be careful, you understand. . . ."

Abelard lifted his shoulders, "I can't understand. Speak English, then I might."

Steve asked, "My *français,* it is not so good, eh?"

"Terrible," Abelard replied in passable English. "Not only do you not use the proper words, but your accent stinks. It's worse than a Turk's!"

Steve shuddered. There it was again, this accusation that he spoke like a Turk! He leaned forward.

"This girl," he spoke in English. "Pretty?"

Abelard kissed his fingertips. "M'sieur, would you call Paris pretty? She is beautiful! A sweet breath of innocence, *charmante . . .*"

The description struck a chord of remembrance. Steve said shrewdly, "Hey, that's almost the same thing my salesmen said! She couldn't be the same girl?"

Abelard was honest, "I told you I knew a young lady well acquainted with your company."

Steve slumped back. "Forget it."

"Why, M'sieur? Because she is intelligent enough to make a good purchase? M'sieur, if I were in your position, I should make an alliance with one not only brilliant but beautiful! I would not seek ill will by fighting!"

Steve flared, "Business is business!"

"Ah, you Americans, one moment so generous, the next so cold. It leads to unhappy international relations. You are a huge corporation. She is a sweet innocent, a rare flower, a young virgin without family! I can just see how my friend, the journalist Raoul Germaine, would love to write his headlines in our prominent newspapers. 'American Octopus Fights Poor Innocent . . . !' "

"Just a minute," Steve protested. "Who said anything about fighting her?"

Abelard shrugged. Steve pondered a moment. A headline like that would be shattering to the corporate image.

"This girl . . . did I hear you say she was a young virgin without family . . ."

Abelard nodded, "M'sieur, I would not offer to introduce you to just *any* kind of a girl!"

Steve held out a hand. "Forget what I said about introductions by taxicab drivers."

Abelard shook his hand. "M'sieur! Never have I made the acquaintance of a more sympathetic American!"

Both men beamed at each other, and Abelard turned the taxi around a corner, just a block away from La Tête.

XLVII

JACQUELINE's outlook on life remained essentially naive. True, the orbit of her friendship had been expanding, as had her cultural outlook. Vassily, who continually popped in and out of her apartment ostensibly to report on his progress in locating Vishevsky, found her a most willing listener as he spoke of the values of objets d'art. He delighted her with the history of Toulouse-Lautrec, who was at ease only with cancan dancers, and women of—er—ah—a more ancient profession. He had hinted that there was a good deal of one aspect of Toulouse in him, and almost fell through the floor when Jacqueline quite candidly reminded him that art was merely a sideline for her, and would become involved in bed only to augment her dowry. Vassily took one look at Pierre's photograph and fled.

Throughout the past few months, Pierre had seen more of the wall than the apartment. Outside of a little yellowing of the emulsion, Abelard once had remarked, Pierre's photograph seemed none the worse for wear. Of course, the wire from which it hung was becoming somewhat frayed, and this Vassily had noticed. On the pretext of replacing this wire, Vassily gathered up his courage to return to the apartment. Jacqueline was pleased that he was so thoughtful, and permitted him to rehang the photograph. While he was so engaged, Abelard arrived with Steve. Vassily was extremely annoyed when Abelard suggested that he leave, despite the fact that Steve expressed delight at meeting a prominent art dealer.

Jacqueline listened gravely as Abelard explained that M'sieur Stanley required to learn the French language. She was rather hesitant about giving lessons, but when she heard that Steve was the vice-president of the company which had built her machine, she frankly and happily welcomed him into her circle. Abelard suggested they open a bottle of wine, at Steve's expense, of course, to mark the conclusion of this arrangement.

Steve cleared his throat, looking meaningfully at Abelard, "Errr!"

Abelard gazed at him uncomprehendingly. Steve motioned him to a corner to confer. Jacqueline complacently went to a record player which she had purchased, and turned on some music. It played softly, and she wriggled in time to the music. Steve could not remove his eyes from her sensuous motion. Abelard called him back from his joy.

"You are not satisfied?"

"Not satisfied?" Steve repeated. "Yes, I think I am, but I haven't quite followed the arrangement." Abelard remained an interested listener. "You said the best way to learn is to live with the girl." Abelard nodded. "Well, what I don't understand is, do I stay here with her, get another apartment, or what?"

Abelard thought a moment, then shrugged, "I forgot to speak to her about that. But does it matter?"

"Of course it matters. We should have a complete understanding at the beginning, not later."

"We-ell," replied Abelard, "this is a matter that requires discussion. I shall speak to Jacqueline."

"Never mind," Steve's haste caused Abelard to arch his eyebrows. "This is a delicate matter that a third party shouldn't be involved in. I'll speak to her ... *alone!*"

"You are suggesting that I leave?"

"Not suggesting ... *telling!*"

Abelard shrugged. Steve dug into his pocket and came forth with a fistful of currency. He tore off two notes and thrust them into Abelard's hand. Abelard glanced at the notes, eyes wide. Steve shoved another note into his hand. Abelard grinned and declared, "Now I know I am going to like you!"

Whistling cheerily, he waved at Jacqueline and departed. Jacqueline waved back and continued wriggling to the music. Steve contemplated her a moment, pausing to absorb the shapeliness of first this part of her anatomy and then that. She turned to him.

"You like to dance?"

He nodded. She held out her arms. He took her in his. They danced. The music stopped. Steve felt the heat coursing through his veins. He held her tightly. She broke away from him.

"Er—" he stammered, "I hope I haven't offended you."

Jacqueline smiled, "You cannot offend me by dancing. You dance very well."

"Look," he blurted, "I'm trying to get something straight between us. You see, Abelard told me he was going to arrange for us to live together."

"So?" Her expression was one of utter innocence and faith in Steve.

"Good Lord!" he exploded. "You act like this is an everyday occurrence."

"No, M'sieur, it is definitely not an everyday occurrence. I have never allowed a man to live with me, either for French lessons, or to be his mistress."

The smattering of Puritan upbringing which Steve possessed, shuddered within him.

"Mistress?"

"That is the arrangement, is it not?" she proceeded calmly. "You are to remain with me to learn our language. You will pay all living expenses, buy me gifts, and recompense me at the end of each week with payments to be established."

"You mean, *here*?"

"Oh, no," she said. "This is my place of business. You have your work, is it not so?"

He nodded.

"You go to your office in the morning, and return when?"

"Oh, whenever I think I'm not needed there."

"Fine. That way I shall be able to arrange my other business with ease."

"You mean, sell those paintings?"

"Of course."

Steve contemplated the room. His gaze stopped on Pierre. He frowned.

Jacqueline went over to the photograph. "You must agree to one more thing. No jealousy, no emotion. This is purely a matter of arrangement between us, nothing more. If it goes beyond business, our agreement is canceled."

"Suppose you should happen to fall in love with me?"

"Impossible. I am already engaged to be married." She indicated the picture, "Pierre, my fiancé."

Steve stared at the picture, "Oh, the man for whom you are purchasing the machine!"

Jacqueline nodded. Steve sighed.

"All right, I promise not to become emotionally entangled."

"And I promise to make you speak French like a native."

Solemnly she held out her hand. Equally as solemn, he shook it. Then, impulsively, she kissed him, and laughed. "Come on, I want you to meet everybody in La Tête!" She took his hand and gaily led him out of the apartment.

Pierre continued to scowl.

XIX

JACQUELINE embraced the arrangement as naturally as the acceptance of a sunrise. Another woman might have pondered the conceit of the male ego expressed in his query, "Suppose you should happen to fall in love with me?"

Jacqueline knew that she could only be constant in her promise to marry Pierre. She had pledged her troth, and that was that. From the time she was old enough to hold a doll, she understood that one day she woud marry a man in her natal community. Proximity and her upbringing had been the catalysts in the natural selection of Pierre. Love, in the passionate, romantic sense, had never been a measure of her future as a wife. It was a cool and calculated decision on her part to go to Paris for a year.

Despite this, her warmth of heart, her unassuming innocence recalled lost vigor, forgotten dreams and the brightness of love to all who came to know her. To the men who knew her, she was more than a desirable woman. She was a thoughtful, sincere and delightful friend.

Jacqueline was content to leave things as they were happening. Her arrangement with the young American was just another association which would guarantee the achievement of her goal. The fact that she could have asked the same question of Steve never entered her thoughts. True, there had been expressions of love murmured into her well-formed ears, but they had been fleeting. She understood that all her clients respected her motivation for being in Paris, and would never consider vowing a love eternal.

Still there existed something about the American that stirred her emotionally. He was a most comfortable man to be with and to keep house for. Shortly after he met all her friends at La Tête, he moved from the George Cinq to a pension

not far from the café. Within a few weeks, Jacqueline felt
that this was impractical. Steve was paying the rent for her
apartment. He had insisted on having a telephone installed.
He had purchased a television set as well as a beautiful
record player. There were other small luxuries that he provided. Each time he called on her, he brought another gift.
Since the pension he lived in had only one bath, and that
one very ancient, he showered in Jacqueline's apartment every
day, sometimes even twice a day.

"Twice a day?" Abelard marveled.

Jacqueline nodded firmly.

"And," Henri the Egg asked for confirmation, "you eat
all your meals with him?"

"Those I do not prepare, we eat here, you all know
that."

Solan nodded. "Your American is a discerning man. He
appreciates my cuisine. You know, only last night he told
me ..."

Michel interrupted, "Yeah, we know ... you have better
cooking than Tour d'Argent!"

Flic sniffed, "A hundred times you've told us!"

Abelard smacked the table, "Silence! We haven't got all
day to advise our little girl!"

"Well," continued Jacqueline, "two people, together, why
should we have two establishments? Why cause this added
expense?"

The taxi men considered this thoughtfully.

The Duke shrugged, "Spoken like a thrifty Frenchwoman;
but after all, you have other things to take care of. You
can't have this American hanging around all the time."

"That's just it," Jacqueline pointed out. "He isn't around
all day. He goes to his business first thing in the morning.
Then, he returns in the evening. Sometimes quite late. Why
should he waste his money on that pension?"

"If," boomed Tiny, "he were just an ordinary tourist, I'd
say who cares what he spends."

"But," declared Abelard, "he is not simply an ordinary
tourist. He wants to be as French as onion soup."

"There is only one drawback," drawled the Duke. All ears
waited to hear what the rotund "adviser" had to say. He
paused to fill a glass from a decanter. He held up the drink
to admire its reflected color.

"A man who lives with a woman cannot help but develop

a sense of proprietorship. Some say it is love, others habit, but it is more a sense of being an Oriental." He paused to let this sink in, expectantly awaiting an inquiry concerning "Oriental." However, the others remained mute, knowing that the Duke would explain without undue urging.

"It is," he philosophized, "a matter of pride for a man to look upon the woman he lives with as his own, for his own use, and for no others. He may bed a different woman every night—but his own woman, what must she do? I'll tell you. She must keep her bed warm only for him. If she doesn't, then he loses pride—"face," the Orientals call it—and we have crimes of passion, suicides, beatings..."

Jacqueline snorted in a dainty manner. "Phoo! You are making a complete drama of a simple arrangement. I am not afraid of these crimes of passion you are dreaming up."

"Of course you are not afraid," the Duke replied. "The woman should never be afraid. The husband, the lover, whoever surprises his woman in somebody else's arms never kills the woman. He shoots the helpless man. He calls upon a law that is unwritten, to cheat the guillotine. Magnanimously, he forgives his woman and she gratefully hurls herself into his arms with renewed passion!"

Jacqueline squealed with laughter. The men stared at her in puzzlement. She continued to laugh.

"Oh," she gasped, "it is like a cinema! Perhaps outside the snow should be falling, and the woman should be running from bloodhounds! You men! All your lives in Paris, and seeing *all* of Paris, yet seeing nothing! A woman of sense arranges her time so that she is not discovered in bed, at least not by a jealous husband. Otherwise, half the male population would be slaughtered every afternoon!" She composed herself, uttering seriously, "In any event, my American is not a child of emotion. He knows I am engaged, and respects my engagement to Pierre."

The Duke shrugged as though washing his hands of the whole affair. Abelard slammed his hand on the table.

"It is a thing most practical! With only one establishment between them, there will be a saving of money which should be Jacqueline's!"

All nodded in agreement, for this was most sensible. Abelard smiled at Jacqueline, "This is an arrangement not proper for a young girl to introduce. I shall discuss it with your American."

Jacqueline smiled thankfully.

"Solan," her voice tinkled, "after such a conference, one becomes hungry and thirsty. A little food and wine for my friends!" She opened her purse and took out some currency, "My treat."

XX

AT FIRST Steve was rather nettled when Abelard broached the subject of his moving into Jacqueline's apartment. He even rather resented Abelard's remark that two could live more cozily together than alone and apart. However, when Jacqueline admitted that it was what she wanted, his last trace of Puritanism curled up its toes and faded away. After all, as she pointed out, he would have more time for his French lessons.

About ten days after he had taken up residence in Jacqueline's apartment, Steve felt it was time for a celebration —a sort of housewarming, as it were. Jacqueline thought this was a splendid idea, provided that the celebration be held in La Tête.

It was quite a party, and Solan, for once, was delighted to see the wine flow. After all, Jacqueline's American was paying for it all. He would have liked to join in the dancing, but there was no one else he could trust to watch the till.

"Dance! Dance! Dance!" Everybody clapped hands. Jacqueline undulated toward Steve, dancing around him. He stumbled, knocked down a table, and grabbed her in his arms. But she slipped away, her eyes challenging him as though to a battle of the sexes. With surprising grace, he looped an arm around her waist and whispered, "Come on! Let's turn Pierre's face to the wall!"

"Aha! Ha!" They all cheered as Steve swept her up from her feet, and charged out of La Tête. Michel picked up a bottle of wine and poured some of the grape down his throat, then hurled the bottle away.

"Michel!" Solan was shocked. "Such breakage! Who will pay for it?"

Michel shrugged, "Add a few francs to the American's bill whenever he comes in."

Abelard's voice was gruff, "*Salauds*! The American is among us a friend! Why cheat him when he is always willing to give us a treat!"

Michel was contrite, "I apologize! I shall break nothing else today!" He snapped his fingers at the musicians, and began to dance by himself.

At that moment, Vassily entered, dragging in a forlorn figure wrapped in old clothes. A greasy knitted cap was pulled tightly down on its head, and a long scarlet scarf entwined its neck.

"Gentlemen!" Vassily's voice throbbed with the emotion of a conqueror. "I have found Vishevsky!"

The music stopped. Michel almost fell. Abelard and the others stared.

The woebegone artist's unshaven, wan face bore an expression of utter meekness and bewilderment. He clutched a rolled canvas tightly in one hand. His other hand fumbled at the scarf to keep it from falling away from his scrawny neck. It was apparent that he was shirtless underneath his tattered coat. He shrank back from the collective gaze of the taxi drivers and the proprietor of La Tête. Solan moaned like a stricken bull.

"Oh, no!"

Abelard laughed, "You wished he was in Siberia!" He jerked a thumb toward Vishevsky, "So you could get your claws on the money Jacqueline's been saving for him!"

Solan struck back, "It's unfair! For more than a year he never paid me a sou for rent or food! You had me at a disadvantage when I agreed to take only a small share of the money from the paintings!"

The taxi men shifted uneasily. Vishevsky stepped forward timorously, "Your pardon, my patron, but I did not come here to ask for money."

Solan whipped at the artist, "Since when am I your patron?"

Vishevsky smiled gently, "You were the first to understand my genius. Why else would you accept my paintings in payment for my living?"

Solan was flattered. He stood straighter and nodded. Vishevsky struck again.

"And—and—when I heard it was here I was to be brought, I decided to bring you a gift!"

With a snap, he unrolled the painting in his hand. It was a series of colorful blotches with semblances of wings repeated over and over again. Solan stared at it in horror. Vassily glanced at it and shut his eyes, but quickly turned to Solan, "If you don't want it, I'll buy it!"

"Who said I don't!"

Hastily, he took the painting from Vishevsky, who licked his dry lips and said, "One good gift deserves another."

Solan sighed, "All right. Help yourself to some wine."

"A moment!" Vassily stopped the artist. "You can start drinking *after* I introduce you to Jacqueline."

The Duke stepped forward, "That is an introduction that will have to wait. Jacqueline is occupied with another matter, so let's relax."

Vishevsky grinned and tugged free of the art dealer's restraining hand. He went behind the bar, and indiscriminately selected several bottles of wine. He set them on the bar, and quickly opened one. Without benefit of a glass, he threw his head back, pursing his lips against the mouth of the bottle, and gulped. The only movement visible was the bobbing of his Adam's apple. The others watched in fascination. Michel softly uttered, "Chug-chug-chug-chug . . ." in time with the bobbing movement. When Vishevsky put down the bottle, he emitted a tremendous burp, and wiped his mouth. Bliss was evident in every line of his face.

Flic sniffed loudly, "Half a bottle! Without a breath!"

The others nodded in admiration. Vishevsky pointed to another bottle, "Join me!"

Solan turned to Vassily, "How much—how much can you get me for this painting?" He held up the canvas.

Vassily shrugged, "Who knows? But I—I am willing to invest not more than a couple of hundred francs."

Solan seemed disappointed. Abelard turned to him.

"Don't be a fool. The clients of Jacqueline will pay more than double!"

Vishevsky, whose abject appearance was melting under the mellowness of the wine, shouted, "Drink! Drink to me, Vishevsky! I have been discovered! Crowds gather to see my paintings!" He tossed more wine down his gullet. "My beautiful, beautiful oils!" He pointed dramatically at the one Solan held, "And that is my last canvas!"

Vassily wheeled, filled with apprehension, "What? Just beginning and already you retire?"

"Who said anything about retiring! It's only from canvas I abstain! My medium is bathtubs! Nothing but bathtubs!" He drank. "You can paint them! You can fill them with vodka! You can sleep in them! Bathtubs! Ah!"

He drained the bottle and dropped it from his hand. Tears welled in his eyes and dribbled down his cheeks.

"*Och te dolye!* Oh, my empty life!" he sobbed. "I am much too happy! I am sure that I am destined to die young!"

He dropped his head into his hands and cried as though the world were coming to an end. The others were stunned.

"Hey, Rushky!" The Duke slammed a hand on the artist's back, "Stop with the Moscow art and get on with the vodka!"

"Vodka?" Vishevsky looked up, his eyes shining. The Duke pushed a bottle toward him.

"*Och te dolye!*" the bathtub genius moaned. "Life is a prison! We break through the bars but only to have them close in!" He quaffed from the bottle.

The Duke glanced at Abelard, shrugging, "These goddam Russians! Show them the road to prosperity and they start crying that they're being cheated!"

"The only reason that Russian's crying," Abelard pointed to Vishevsky, "is that being discovered means he may have to work!"

"Gentlemen! Please! Please!" Vassily begged. "I didn't find him to get him drunk! He must see Jacqueline!"

Vishevsky emptied another bottle and continued to weep.

XXI

THE RISE of Vishevsky from obscurity created a being who was at one time filled with insufferable arrogance, and then with almost quicksilver rapidity became a creature of abject slavery. The money he received from Jacqueline was more than he had ever held in his hand during all his existence.

From a misbegotten concept that clothes make the man, he immediately splurged on an outlandish conglomeration of sports clothes, caps and berets of vivid hues. Although he changed his clothes frequently, he never washed more than his face and hands. Bathtubs, he believed, were not to be despoiled by soap and water. After Vassily obtained him the first commission from Binet, Vishevsky's fame soared, from the Left Bank to the Right.

All Paris wanted bathtubs painted by Vishevsky. With this clamor for nudes à la Vishevsky, the mantle of celebrity began to drape itself on his shoulders. To say that it went to his head was vast understatement. The wrinkles were out of his belly, and he had suddenly blossomed forth as a gourmet. Unfortunately for Solan, Vishevsky's "gourmetmanship" consisted chiefly of rude criticism. *This* was underdone! *That* lacked sufficient saffron! The meat was tough! The salads were limp! And the wines were flat! The truth was that he felt he could overcome his ignorance of gracious living by belittling everything he could now afford to buy.

However, if Jacqueline was present, Vishevsky bowed and scraped. He spoke in reverent tones, and even a stale piece of bread left him grateful. He took every opportunity to be in her company, grating on Steve's nerves to the point where the American decided it was time to eliminate the artist from the scene. He found natural allies in the taxi drivers of La Tête.

"I remember a cinema," Solan suggested, "this irritating *cochon* of a newfound fortune offended the owner of a night club. They put him in a cement mixer and paved a road with him. I think that . . ."

"No," said Abelard, "that would be too drastic."

"Hey," said Flic brightly, "wine should do it. We get him drunk and push him into a wine vat and drown him."

Alsace grumbled, "Why spoil good wine." Tiny, who was enjoying some tea which he poured into a saucer to drink, rumbled between slurping sips, "It appears that our American friend," he indicated Steve, "should come right out and tell Jacqueline that they don't need a Russian lapdog running in and out of their apartment at all hours."

Steve shrugged. It was a very Gallic shrug, revealing how strong was the influence of his companions and environment. "Don't you think I've hinted at it? I've even almost demanded the removal of that stinking Vishevsky. But you know Jacqueline. She doesn't even see the harm in a cockroach!"

"I've made up my mind," Solan was firm. "I don't care

if Jacqueline's with him or not, he says one word for or against my sauces, I'll garrote him!"

"And be guillotined?" The Duke shook his head, "No, no violence. There is only one way to eradicate this nuisance, a bathtub!"

Steve exploded, "This bane came into existence through bathtubs! Everywhere I go, people talk about him and his bathtubs!"

"Not Jacqueline."

Steve admitted, "Strangely enough, not Jacqueline." Abelard studied the Duke, and suddenly caught a glimmer in his eye.

"Hah!" Abelard sounded like a man who had seen the light. The Duke grinned at Abelard, whose face shone with anticipation.

"Our minds are similar, eh, Abelard?"

Abelard chuckled, "Only there is Jacqueline to overcome."

The rotund cab driver continued to speak to Abelard as though no others were present.

"It is time she had a small vacation. A weekend, I believe that can be arranged by Steve."

"What the hell are you two conniving?" Steve demanded.

The two cabbies ignored him. "You think a weekend will be long enough?"

The Duke rubbed his belly, "Why not? It isn't a very large bathtub."

Henri the Egg leaned forward, "I know. We force him to take a bath!"

Abelard and the Duke chuckled.

"That," the Duke slapped Abelard's shoulder, "that would be the cherry atop the charlotte russe!"

Steve howled, "I can't follow this mental telepathy you two engage in! Better fill me in, step by step!"

Abelard smiled indulgently. "Since you will be with Jacqueline, it is better you know nothing."

The Duke nodded, "All we require is that you take Jacqueline on a little weekend trip. When you return, Vishevsky will wish he had never heard of a bathtub!"

"And that," the Duke suggested, "calls for you to gratefully invite us all to split a bottle of wine!"

Steve sighed. He was always gratefully inviting them to have some wine. But this time he felt he was getting his money's worth.

XXII

JACQUELINE BUBBLED OVER with girlish delight when Steve suggested that they explore the French countryside for the weekend. He felt a twinge of guilt at her purely innocent acceptance of what he knew was a keystone of a devious plan to get rid of Vishevsky.

But the beauty of the French countryside, the joy of being alone with this girl of girls dissipated any qualms he may have possessed.

For the first time he took note of the well-groomed poplars along the roads, and the strange plants nestling in the branches of the trees.

"Mistletoe," Jacqueline informed him.

"Mistletoe!" he cried and steered directly under the nearest tree. "Who has to wait for Christmas!" He embraced her in a passionate kiss. She laughed happily as she gently withdrew from him.

"Look," he pointed, "there's miles and miles of mistletoe!"

Jacqueline's laughter was like a silver bell in a summer's breeze. "Ah, but I shall not yield to mile upon mile of kisses. Not here on the open road at any rate!"

He grinned. They still had a long drive toward the seacoast which was their destination.

Steve would always remember that weekend. Just below the small inn where they stayed they could see the fishermen mending their nets as fishermen had done on this coast for a hundred years. When they strolled along the beach, hand in hand, people greeted them warmly, smiling at them as people only smiled at young lovers.

It was with heartfelt regret that Steve said adieu to this idyllic seacoast.

In the moonlight, the road to Paris appeared to be a long band of silver expertly beaten out to dwindle in the dark horizon of earth meeting sky. The glowing night suffused Jacqueline's profile with a tender loveliness that made Steve's heart ache with emotion. He felt like a poet speaking to his love, and her reply was a murmur of happy contentment.

It would be wonderful, he thought, if these two days could be stretched into a lifetime. His eyes caressed her face, drank in the purity of her throat, the rise and fall of her perfectly formed breasts, the swell of her womanly hips. She glanced at him through the veil of her thick lashes as his hand fell on the softness of her legs.

"Attend the road, Steve, or we shall not get home to our bed in one piece."

He pulled his hand away and fastened his eyes to the silvery ribbon before them. For some unknown reason, the features of Pierre formed in his mind.

"Damn Pierre!" he uttered through clenched teeth.

She sat upright, staring at him in consternation.

He saw her out of the corner of his eyes.

"Do you realize," he declared, "that for two days you and I have been together without once having to look at his ugly face!"

She shrugged, reminding him that he had no right to object to her devotion to Pierre.

The remainder of the journey home was accomplished in silence. However, when they halted in front of the apartment, Steve was contrite. He was also hungry. He dropped her off and went around to La Tête to buy a couple of bottles of wine and some sandwiches.

Solan greeted Steve effusively, as though he had been gone for a year. He took Steve's order, announcing that he was happy that the American and Jacqueline had returned. Since their absence, he hadn't seen much of Abelard, the Duke and Vishevsky, and business had been unusually dull.

"By the bye," he wondered, picking up a small chit, "that Abelard, he ordered five bottles of vodka and some wine which he said you would pay for."

Steve studied the chit. Before he could answer, Jacqueline burst in.

"Steeeeeeve!" she wailed. "Something terrible has happened!"

She flung herself into his arms, tears streaking her cheeks. Steve caressed her head.

"There, there, *chérie*, calm yourself. What is it that is so terrible?"

"In the apartment! Come!"

She clasped his hand and virtually dragged him along with her.

XXIII

"BURGLARS!"

Steve stared at the disarray of the apartment. The bed was rumpled. There was a wall-to-wall litter of empty vodka bottles, paint-smeared rags and paper. It appeared to him that extremely untidy burglars had ransacked the place during their absence.

"Not burglars," Jacqueline moaned. "I wish it had been burglars!"

She pointed dramatically toward the slightly open door of the bathroom.

"In there!"

Steve tiptoed to the bathroom. He swiftly flattened himself against the wall, as he had seen done by heroes of the motion picture screen. Then, he deftly kicked open the door and jumped inside the bathroom, shouting, "Don't move! I've got you covered!"

He came to an abrupt halt, mouth and eyes agape like bewildered O's.

"Holy Jehoshaphat!" he screeched. "It's a dead body!"

Jacqueline shuddered. "Dead, yes. Dead drunk!" She kicked indignantly at an expired vodka bottle on the floor. Steve bent down for a closer perusal of the body sprawled in the tub. He laughed in relief.

"Why, it's Vishevsky! What's so tragic and terrible? He's only sleeping it off!"

Jacqueline pointed in misery, "If he were drunk ten times over, I wouldn't care, but look *what* he is asleep on!"

Steve bent closer and gasped. "Good Lord! It's one of his nudes!"

"Painted forever in my bathtub!" Jacqueline shuddered, her voice lowered to a labored whisper. "And every detail, if you will notice, very identifiable!"

Steve pushed the sleeping drunk to one side, and released him immediately, as though he were a hot coal. He turned to stare at Jacqueline, whose misery was as great as ever.

"It appears more like myself than myself," she moaned. He patted her sympathetically.

"Never mind, we'll toss him out on his butt, and we'll get some turpentine or something and erase it."

"It will do no good!" Jacqueline suddenly was transformed from her misery to a grim and determined Amazon. "There is a secret in his paint that makes it permanent, but I have had a sudden and horrible thought!"

Steve was at a loss to discern her meaning.

"Those other bathtubs! *Whose* face do you suppose he painted in them!"

Without further ado, she turned on all faucets full blast. The minor Niagara burst onto the limp Vishevsky like the greatest of medieval tortures. He sprang up, like a man embraced by a reclining Iron Maiden, and spluttered and gasped for breath. Jacqueline pushed at him and he slipped back into the tub, the water beating at him. He howled.

"Murderers! I am drowning!"

"Drown, then," Jacqueline howled back. "You ingrate! You sneak in artist's clothing!"

Steve tried to pull Jacqueline back, but she wriggled free and grabbed a long-handled scrubbing brush and began pounding Vishevsky on the head. The "drowning" artist managed to get hold of the shower faucets, frantically drawing himself to his feet. The soap slid out of its container and fell into the tub, just as Vishevsky stepped down. He skittered, he slid, he lost his hold on the shower, twisting the faucet knobs, and water shot down in every direction. Down went Vishevsky, dragging Jacqueline with him.

"Aughhh!" Vishevsky gasped.

"Gleeeopov!" Jacqueline gargled.

"Holy Jehoshaphat!" Steve cried, as he fumbled for all the faucets, getting just as wet as the two bathers before he could shut off the downpour. He helped Jacqueline, whose coiffure consisted of wet and matted hair, out of the tub, tossing her a long towel to cover her soaked, clinging dress.

"Better dry yourself and get into something else before you catch pneumonia!" he ordered. Meekly, Jacqueline left the bathroom.

Steve shut the door to give her privacy, then collared Vishevsky and hauled him from the tub. Water dripped from Vishevsky's hair, his eyes, his mouth, his clothes and his shoes. He moaned and gasped.

"Water! I am covered with water! I am filled with water!"

"That," pointed out Steve dryly, "usually happens when you take a bath, especially in your clothes."

"A bath?" Vishevsky was bewildered. "I was taking a bath?"

"Sure," said Steve solemnly. "You were so drunk you didn't know what you were doing."

Vishevsky sat down on the edge of the tub, befuddled and weary. He shook his head, "A bath! I was taking a bath! I must really have been drunk!"

"And were you drunk when you painted that?" Steve pointed accusingly at the latest Vishevsky nude.

"Ah!" Vishevsky's face was a study in admiration. "She is beautiful, no? She is my masterpiece, yes? I have never done better. All my other bathtubs are as nothing!"

He stood up straight, wringing out his clothes.

"Jacqueline will be proud!" His face squinched up in thought, "Jacqueline! She was in here with you, no?"

Steve grinned, "You better ask her that yourself."

He knocked on the door, "Sweetie, may we come out?"

Jacqueline called back, "No! I'm coming in!"

As good as her word, she came in, a towel wrapped around her body, another around her head.

"Ah," said Vishevsky, "to show my gratitude, I have made you immortal!" He flung a hand out toward the bathtub.

"And," Jacqueline purred like a tigress ready to pounce on her prey, "in how many bathtubs have you made me immortal?"

Vishevsky preened, all unsuspecting of his imminent doom.

"From the very first, I had in my mind your sort of shapeliness, texture of skin, coloring. In this very room, I created a semblance of your beauty, but when I saw you, my imagination came into full bloom. You made my original nude pale by comparison. Certainly, I have since painted many bathtubs—but none, none so perfect as this one!"

Pridefully, he patted the bathtub.

"So!" Jacqueline's hazel eyes were threatening slits, "I am on display in bathrooms all over Paris!" She flung her arms wide. The towel loosened around her torso. Frantically, Steve clawed at the towel, managing to grab it before it displayed any portion of Jacqueline. She pushed his hands away, and turned her full fury on the artist.

"I befriended you! I saved money for you! I had pity

for you! And you repay me with treachery! I shall be ashamed to be seen anywhere! People will point and say, there she is, the girl who is undressed in everybody's bathtub! Even her own!"

"But, *ma petite,*" Vishevsky protested, "I paint you with love, with beauty, with . . ."

"With paint that is indelible!" Jacqueline cried. "And until you are able to eliminate this—this—shameful atrocity," her finger trembled as it aimed dramatically into her bathtub, "get out of my sight, and stay out!"

She whipped about and haughtily strode into the apartment. Vishevsky turned a tortured face to Steve.

"*Och te dolye!* I only did this to please her. The Duke and Abelard assured me that . . ."

Swiftly, Steve clapped his hand over Vishevsky's mouth, hissing, "Jacqueline doesn't have auburn hair for nothing! You say another word, and she'll really lose her temper! And Lord knows what she might do to you then!"

The artist's eyes bugged. Steve whispered swiftly, "Better get out like she said, or you may wind up back in that tub, soaked, soaped and scrubbed to the skin!"

He released Vishevsky, whose expression was filled with horror. He shuddered as he glanced back at the tub, then with a moan he stumbled out of the bathroom, blindly found the apartment's exit, and disappeared.

Grinning happily, Steve approached Jacqueline who was sitting on the bed, trying to comb her knotted hair.

"You were magnificent! Simply magnificent!"

She said nothing. He sat down next to her and took the comb from her hair and gently began to run it through her tresses. The towel had slipped down, baring her shoulders.

"Steve," her voice was sad, "perhaps I should not have lost my temper."

"You were justified in getting rid of him."

"Ah, but of what good is it? I have not got rid of that painting!"

He kissed her bared shoulder tenderly, "There are other bathtubs—all sorts of bathtubs I can buy you."

She sighed, "It appears that in all of France, I am the only one who changes bathtubs as frequently as my lingerie!"

He continued to kiss her bare shoulders, then her neck, finally he had her in his arms and kissed her lips, his hand seeking her bare flesh.

"No, no, Steve!" She wriggled free of his embrace, "Not now! We mustn't!"

"Why not?" he demanded. "We're alone at last!"

"We are not alone!"

She gestured toward the wall. Steve glared. The photograph of Pierre glared back at him.

Jacqueline was right. They were not alone. He stood up, his mind whirling. He had gotten rid of Vishevsky. Pierre would have to go! He riveted angry eyes upon the photograph. The photograph leered back at him.

Jacqueline touched Steve's face and turned it to her. She smiled tenderly. Ah, he was so like a little boy deprived of his chocolate. She kissed him lightly and reached up and turned Pierre's face to the wall.

XXVI

THE DUKE spun his cab crazily around Place Vendôme, madly honking the horn. Abelard, about to accept a passenger, came to attention. The Duke leaned out and shouted:

"A crisis! *Allons!*"

Hastily, Abelard slammed the door of his taxi in the surprised face of the almost passenger, and sped after the Duke, adding the tootle of his horn to that of the Duke's. They wove through the traffic at top speed, overtaking Tiny, who already had a passenger. They gesticulated wildly. Tiny immediately pulled over to the curb and ordered the passenger to descend. The man protested, but Tiny merely reached in and lifted him to the sidewalk.

Along Boulevard Haussmann, down and around to the Place de la République, the entourage sped and grew, adding to its collection Alsace, Henri the Egg and Michel.

The Duke shouted, "If we do not find Flic in the next five minutes, rendezvous at the Café des Poissonniers!"

The cabs headed in different directions, searching for Flic.

In a city of traffic normally maniacal, these drivers appeared to be escaped bedlamites. Their taxis scurried down this street and that, darting deftly around pedestrians, shooting past sundry vehicles, leaving hot tempers and frightened drivers behind them. There was no sign of Flic. As zero hour approached, the taxis all headed for the Café des Poissonniers, a small coffee house sandwiched by a fly-infested *boucherie chevaline* and an equally pest-ridden fruit stand. The tattered awning of the café hung limply over several tables. A huge-busted woman, sweaty and bemustached, rolled out of the café to them.

"Aha!" her voice was like a cow horn, "Solan has finally exterminated you!"

"Madame," Abelard replied coldly, "we came here for coffee and contemplation, not conversation."

The woman shook with anger. "With customers like you, I'll go to the poorhouse!" She turned and pointed to a fly specked sign. "Observe, that is the rule of the house!"

They observed.

"So," shrugged Abelard, "you have always announced a minimum of three francs for those occupying tables."

"I make this announcement again to you because unless you make it profitable for me to serve you, go and contemplate somewhere else."

The Duke stood up and put his arm around the woman's shoulders. He tweaked her multiple chins, "Ah, you grow more and more beautiful. Bring us coffee, and let us get on with our business. Afterwards, you and I—we will talk of more intimate things, *hein*?"

The woman simpered, "For you, yes. . . . but *only* for you!" She turned, taking mincing little steps that shook her ample bottom. The Duke sighed. Abelard grinned.

"One of these days, my Cossack lover, you will be trapped by her and be compelled to deliver!"

The Duke shivered, "On that day remind me to be a corpse."

Alsace glanced at his watch, "We are losing money by the second. Get on with the crisis!"

"Yeah," rumbled Tiny. "It better be worth my kicking out a paying passenger."

The Duke signaled for discretion. The fat proprietress bore down on them with a large tray of overslopping coffee cups. The Duke jumped up and took the tray from her.

"Here, this is too much for so dainty a woman!"

She simpered. She minced. She shook. She started to pull up a chair. The Duke patted her rump.

"In this bright sunshine, the delicacy of your skin might be destroyed."

"Oh," her hand touched her overblown cheeks, "you are the most thoughtful of men."

She glanced at him archly, and returned to the interior of her café, wiggling her posterior which was of a size that only an Ottoman could admire.

Abelard grinned. He shook a finger at the Duke. "She dangles ample bait, my fine, thoughtful man; but remember the trap!"

The Duke shuddered and passed the coffee around.

"All I can remember is what Jacqueline confided in me a short while ago." He paused to see if he had the attention of all. "La Tête is to be rated in the *Golden Gourmet Guide!*"

"That's wonderful," Henri the Egg beamed. "It will improve Solan's business."

"Wonderful? For Solan's cash register! But not for us!" The Duke leaned forward, "*We* will be *dispossessed!*"

There was a moment of absolute silence.

The Duke continued, "If not for Jacqueline, the Golden Gourmet Society would never have heard of La Tête. She kept reminding Prince Igor of Solan's ambition to be recognized."

"I knew it," Alsace's lugubrious moan accused, "Jacqueline has discovered that you persuaded Vishevsky to paint her bathtub! Now she strikes back!"

"Nothing of the sort," the Duke denied. "Her innocent heart could not stand the yearning of Solan's ambition. Now, today, this morning, Prince Igor has informed her that a Golden Gourmet inspector has been scheduled to dine at La Tête!"

"So?" Henri the Egg blew into his steaming coffee to cool it. "A listing in the guide is not a dispossess notice."

The Duke snorted. "If La Tête gets a good rating, it will become popular. That means crowds. Higher prices. Bigger profits. Bigger profits mean a fancier, more exclusive place with a menu that cannot afford us, nor which we can afford. Therefore, simple inflation will drive us from our position at La Tête."

Abelard began to toy with a spoon. Annoyed, the Duke pulled the spoon from his hand.

"We face a crisis and you play with spoons!"

"I see no crisis," Abelard said mildly. He sipped his coffee and grimaced, "This is like drinking hemlock." He pushed the beverage away and smirked. All attention riveted on him.

"It requires merely to prevent La Tête from losing its

present obscurity." He paused briefly to allow consideration of his wisdom. "That is an achievement of great simplicity. We make certain that the Golden Gourmet inspector fails to enjoy the cuisine at La Tête."

"Ah!" The Duke brightened.

"Aha!" grinned Tiny.

"This coffee," declared Henri the Egg, "already tastes better!"

XXV

JACQUELINE WAS aghast when she discovered the conspiracy against Solan. Naturally, she would not betray her "board of advisers." But she protested vehemently against any action that might hurt Solan's feelings, let alone his pocketbook.

Abelard diplomatically tried to explain that the fortunes of stylish restaurants were as the will-o'-the-wisp. Only a few stood the test of time and the whims of fashion. Customers like themselves were the mainstay of La Tête, regardless of fickle popularity. Indeed, they were doing this for Solan!

"Hmmph!" was her reply.

A pall of gloom settled over the taxi men. Jacqueline had stirred a sympathy for Solan that they had not suspected existed within their hearts. Their collective conscience squirmed at their plot to tamper with Solan's creations.

After all, Jacqueline reminded them, Solan was a man with a dream that could come true. To interfere, would turn that dream into a nightmare to haunt not only Solan, but all of them!

Not to interfere, Abelard pronounced, would merely assure that the comfort of a way of life, which had taken them years to build, would become a thing of the past.

"Perhaps not," Jacqueline persuaded. "Take Solan into your confidence. Tell him the truth. He is more than a sou-saving entrepreneur. He is a friend!"

This was a decision, they agreed, that would have to be mulled over carefully. Until a conclusion had been reached, no one was to inform Solan of the impending visit from the Golden Gourmet representative.

Since these appraisers of food kept their identity secret, Abelard arranged that at least one of the taxi drivers would always be present at La Tête. He was certain that their innate acumen would smell out the "Gee Gee," as they referred to the Golden Gourmet man.

Jacqueline took every opportunity to remind them of their true obligation to Solan. She watched the "watchers" with trepidation, hoping that their basic honesty would prevail, so that Solan would have a fighting chance to achieve the *cordon bleu* or whatever it was that the best restaurants won.

Then, one evening, when business was at a standstill, a little man of inconspicuous mien strolled in. He stood at the bar and hesitantly asked Solan for an aperitif. Abelard and the Duke were the only other customers. They merely glanced at the stranger, who seemed to be a clerk or a bookkeeper or something like that. He quietly tasted his aperitif.

A moment later, Jacqueline hurried in. Seeing the little man, she slowed down, and with studied casualness strolled over to her two friends and sat down. She gazed surreptitiously at the little man, her eyes widening as though she recognized him. Then she leaned forward to the taxi drivers.

"Him! He's here!" she hissed.

"Who?" they wondered.

"Gee Gee!" She tipped her head toward the little man.

Abelard studied him, "How do you know? He looks just like the grocer down the street."

She sniffed disdainfully, "Prince Igor, who knows all about 'Gee Gees,' does not waste telephone calls to describe grocers."

It was obvious from the reaction of Abelard and the Duke that this inside information was more acceptable than their innate acumen.

Jacqueline studied the little man closely. So unprepossessing! Hardly the gourmet type. But, then, one could rarely tell a dish without tasting it. She had imagined that the "Gee Gee" would be an elegant epicure, immaculately tailored, superbly suave, not somebody who could be anybody.

Her eyes rested on Abelard and the Duke, seeming to inquire what they would do. Was their fear of being dispossessed greater than their loyalty to a friend? With her heart in her mouth, she watched them rise slowly, and approach the bar.

"*B'jour*," Abelard greeted the little man, who nodded pleasantly. The Duke smiled at him.

"Would you care to join me in another aperitif?"

"That's exceedingly friendly of you, M'sieur, but *merci*, this one will clarify my taste buds, another may dull them."

The Duke tossed a quick glance at Abelard, who lifted his eyebrows. Solan, absorbed in reading a magazine, paid no attention to them.

"M'sieur, I take it you plan to dine here?" the Duke resumed his conversation.

"I do," replied the little man.

"Then," said the Duke, "permit me to make you comfortable at a cool table."

Jacqueline's heart jumped forward in her mouth. Her temper began to stir. Then, as if she had uttered a silent prayer which was answered with the speed of light, Abelard tapped Solan on the shoulder and got his attention.

"This is an emergency," he hissed. "Follow me!" He gestured toward the kitchen. Solan was too startled to protest. He followed. Unable to stand the suspense, Jacqueline jumped up and hurried after them. She could hear a portion of the Duke's conversation, "*Mon ami,* you have just entered on a new experience. The food, ah! . . . ."

"Shut the door," Abelard said as Jacqueline entered the kitchen, and he spoke quickly to Solan, "Today, you must achieve your sauces and dishes like you have never created them before!"

Solan stared at him, "What makes today so special?"

"That little man. The one out there, he makes it your day of days!"

"Solan," it was Jacqueline, "he is the one who establishes the rating in the *Golden Gourmet Guide!*"

As she spoke, she put down her purse, straightened her dress and took down a small apron hanging nearby.

"A menu, give me a menu."

"Oh, my!" groaned Solan. He trembled in every fiber, "Oh, my!"

"Steady! A straight back, a chin high!" Abelard encouraged. "He is a man like any other man!"

"Oh, my!" Solan collapsed onto a nearby stool. "I shake in every nerve. Look!"

He held his hands out. They seemed to beat a tattoo on the air. "I'll never be able to handle a knife or a ladle with composure! Why didn't you warn me earlier!"

"To tell you the truth," Abelard confessed, "we were considering sabotaging you altogether to protect our headquarters here. But, ah well, friendship means more than a comfortable table."

"And, I tell you," Jacqueline informed, "that a greater sacrifice no group of men has ever made. You must stop quivering like a tub of jelly, and cook like you've never cooked before! Now, where is a menu?"

Solan remained speechless. Abelard turned to Jacqueline, "Go ahead, wait on him, tell him there is no menu. He orders, Solan creates!"

The Duke was regaling the little man with descriptions of the famous banquets depicted by the newspaper clippings on the surrounding walls, apparently with no effect. Jacqueline's arrival, however, put fire into the man's interest.

"May I serve you?" she inquired, as though born to apron and menu.

"Ah," the little man blinked, "ah, I—ah—" His eyes transfixed on her in utter admiration. "The bill of fare. . ."

"There is no menu, whatever you order is prepared as you like."

"Well, I would—like—ah—umm! . . ." His eyes traveled the length and breadth of Jacqueline.

She smiled, realizing her potential influence.

"While you're deciding, perhaps some wine, a Pernod. . ,"

"Pernod?" the little man's voice seemed to be in shock.

"Pernod," Jacqueline repeated, and turned to the bar. It was obvious the little man wished to recall her, but he seemed too embarrassed to do so. Behind the bar, Jacqueline poured the Pernod. She gazed at it uncertainly, then instead of adding water, she added gin. When the little man received the glass, he hesitated a moment, then sipped. A light of astonishment gleamed in his eyes. He sipped again, as if to make certain this was Pernod. Then he took a deep draught and settled back, relaxing for the first time.

"M'selle," he said expansively, "this Pernod *is* Pernod! Never have I tasted so excellent a Pernod!" He finished it.

"Another?" asked Jacqueline. He nodded. Jacqueline returned to the bar, this time deftly mixing gin and Pernod.

But what of the confidence of Solan? There in the kitchen he was rattled and nervous. His hands fumbled with this, and dropped that, until he sank back against a wall to wipe the perspiration from his brow.

"I can't!" he moaned. "I can't do anything right!"

Abelard soothed him, "Never give up, *mon ami!* I, Abelard, will assist you! You create, I will handle the heavy stuff."

He patted Solan on the back, lifted his apron to wipe his brow, and cheered him on to resume his culinary skill.

"You want eggs, I will hand them to you, butter, I will get it. A knife, a mixer, just tell me. You concentrate on the operation."

"Eggs, butter?" Solan shrugged. "What if he orders something that does not require them?"

Abelard patted him on the back, "Regard, you are Solan! No matter what he orders, you serve him a Creation Solan, the specialty of the house!"

Abelard's features brightened like a new dawn, "Hey, that's it. Creation Solan Surprise, specialty of the house!"

He whipped about and opened the kitchen door, beckoning and calling, "M'selle! If you please!"

Jacqueline came to him quickly, holding a glass of gin-Pernod. Abelard whispered to her, "Inform him, he is being served the specialty of the house."

Jacqueline nodded and lifted the glass, "A few more of these and you can serve him toilet water for champagne, and he'd smack his lips!"

"Good girl!" Abelard chucked her under the chin. He turned back to Solan.

"Eggs!"

Abelard handed Solan some eggs. Solan broke them, separated the white from the yolk and began to beat them separately. Without looking up, Solan asked for cream.

"Cream!" Abelard announced, slapping the cream into Solan's hands.

"Measuring spoon!" Solan demanded.

Abelard found the measuring spoon and slapped it into the extended hand. The operation was in progress. Solan was the master surgeon of the culinary arts, Abelard, his willing assistant. Ingredient after ingredient called for was handed to the chef, along with instrument after instrument, and then finally, the ultimate touch—a drop of brandy. Whatever it was, Abelard couldn't tell. It was neither fondue, nor soufflé, it was not a sweet, nor was it a true entrée. It was as he had dubbed it, a surprise. Solan tasted. He offered Abelard a taste.

"Something's missing."

"You think so?" Solan was worried.

"I believe not enough brandy."

Solan shook his head, "Enough brandy. Perhaps champagne." He had an open bottle of champagne. He poured a trifle. Abelard jiggled his elbow. Most of the bottle gushed out. Solan groaned. Abelard tasted.

"Ah, fit for the gods!"

Solan tasted, "Umm. Not bad. Now, it can stand a bit more brandy."

Abelard picked up the bottle and poured. He poured generously. Solan grabbed the bottle from him.

"*Bon Dieu!* This is food for a delicate palate, not a drunkard!"

He mixed, he stirred, he tasted. He tasted again. He beamed. Abelard tasted, he also beamed. From the dining room came a song raised on a pleasant tenor voice.

"Hey!" said Abelard. "What's that?"

Both opened the kitchen door and peered out. The little man was standing on the table dancing and singing, while the Duke pounded his hands together to keep time. Jacqueline turned toward the astonished duo of kitcheneers and waved.

"It's settled, Solan, five knives, forks, stars—whatever it is they give out—you've got it!"

"But," protested Solan, "my surprise creation, he must eat it!"

Jacqueline shrugged, "After this dance, he won't know whether he is eating or swimming. So, surprise yourself!"

Abelard beckoned to her. She came over. "Listen, the surprise surprised even me. Get rid of that great epicure, and join us in the kitchen!"

He bobbed back into the kitchen and began to stuff himself with the dish.

"No!" Solan shouted, "No! We must save some so I can figure out the recipe!"

All Abelard could do was rumble deep in his belly and emit a volcanic belch.

XXVI

TROUBLE WAS brewing at Au Paradis. The fallen angels of that establishment were in a state of revolt. Suzanne, Roxanne and Yvette presented a solid front to Madame Vannois. Jacqueline's success had gone to their heads.

"Regard," declared Suzanne. "She is without the protection of an establishment, and she not only has a rich American, but a following of gentlemen in very high places."

"And," added Roxanne, "through her efforts, La Tête has obtained a formidable reputation for its food!"

Madame Vannois shrugged, "Sooner or later her independence will bring about her downfall. She will be watched closely, and unless she returns to her farmer, she will become an inhabitant of the gutters."

"Perhaps, perhaps not," Suzanne shrugged. "Meantime, she shares her profits only with herself, even to the extent of purchasing a machine of enormous value for her dowry."

"Her extravagance," Madame Vannois snapped, "is no concern of mine!"

She waved her hand, indicating that the audience was over. Though Roxanne and Yvette wavered, Suzanne stood her ground.

"It should be, as it makes us dissatisfied. We have a modest and comfortable income, which affords *no* extravagances, yet affords you any luxury you desire. All we request is another arrangement, so that we, too, may hope for a small portion of such luxury. Otherwise. . ."

"Otherwise what?" Madame Vannois purred ominously.

"We shall follow the example of Jacqueline and establish ourselves independently!"

Ordinarily, Madame Vannois' temper would have flowed like molten lava, but she controlled the eruption with regal aplomb. There had been minor complaints which she had merely brushed aside, but this threatened to be the sort of revolution which could figuratively bring her to the guillotine. For the moment, she was compelled to compromise. Later, when she worked out a plan to destroy Jacqueline and her

116

unwitting aid to open rebellion, her serfs would be happy to beg her forgiveness.

"My dear children," she certainly was the wronged mother, "I always want you to come to me with your problems. We are a family, not merely strangers seeking to take advantage of each other. Of course I have been firm with you, but that was for your benefit. Could I allow you not to know the true value of money? Could I stand by and see you be foolish with your earnings, so that when you should be ready to retire comfortably you would possess nothing and have to depend on charity?"

"*Merde!*"

"Wha—what?" Madame Vannois could not believe her ears.

"You heard me," declared Suzanne. "Stop with the mother act and get on with a new arrangement or we walk."

Madame Vannois drew herself to her full height.

"I will not tolerate such evil language among my girls! However, I realize you have been under an evil influence since you have mentioned this Jacqueline. I forgive you." She paused a moment. "I have every intention of giving you larger shares. Immediately, I cannot tell you how much larger. I shall have Vannois check our books, and before this month is over, report to you the utmost Au Paradis can afford."

The three girls whispered among each other. It was obvious that they had not expected such a quick and easy victory. Their decision was equally as speedy.

Suzanne nodded, "That is acceptable."

They left without waiting to be dismissed.

"Vannois!" Madame called.

The door at the side, leading to her bathroom, opened. Vannois, holding a glass of cognac, popped out.

"You heard?"

Vannois nodded. "When shall I start with the books?"

"Imbecile!" she shouted. "Never!"

He gulped his drink.

"You will concentrate on Jacqueline. She must be eliminated!"

Vannois gawked, "No!"

"Don't argue!"

"I'm not arguing! It's simply a matter of refusing to put our heads under the guillotine!"

It was her turn to gawk, then she laughed as it dawned on her what Vannois believed.

"Idiot!" she laughed. "I said 'eliminate' not 'liquidate!' We must expose Jacqueline to certain parties. There is a law against her kind!"

"That law may hurt us too, *ma petite*."

"Never! We are protected. Au Paradis is a tax-paying establishment selling wines, spirits and entertainment. Jacqueline, why, she has no official standing or position. A word dropped here and another there will finish her."

"It may take some doing," Vannois was dubious. "Meantime our little rebels may become impatient."

"Bah! Let them! I'll handle that!"

Vannois nodded. He glanced at his empty glass and began to head for the liquor cabinet.

"Enough is sufficient, Vannois!"

He halted.

"You will require clarity in that soft brain of yours for the next few days. You will dine at La Tête, get more friendly than you are now with Jacqueline. Learn who she sees, who goes to her place. That is what is known as evidence necessary to destroy her."

Vannois put down his empty glass. This was not work that he preferred, but he knew that it was essential to his present existence. He shrugged sadly.

"Whatever you say, *chérie*, whatever you say."

He turned and left, wondering what he would run into at La Tête, and how he would answer any insults. There was one ray of light in this role of spy. Solan had an excellent selection of alcoholic spirits.

XXVII

HAD JACQUELINE known of the disaster Madame Vannois was plotting for her, she would have paid little attention to it. There had been subtle changes in her philosophy, which were revealed in many little ways. Her relationship with men of the world polished her with a tinge of Parisian sophistication. She was aware of the differences in wines, the nuances of excellent food, the attitudes of persons and personages. She was progressing in growth of outlook without realizing it. Essentially, however, she was still Jacqueline, warm of heart, earthy in her honesty, and firm in her conviction that her destiny was the machine and Pierre. That was the future. Meanwhile, she lived each day for what the day brought. She indulged in certain extravagances, not planned extravagances, but extravagances of impulse. It might be an unusual hat, or a pair of American shoes, perhaps a few ounces of unusual perfume. As generous as she was with herself, she was occasionally even more generous with others. There was the time that Abelard's taxi had a siege of breakdown, which caused him to fall behind in making his payments to the bank. Despite Abelard's reluctance, she insisted on giving him the required funds as a loan which both knew he could never repay. The youngsters of the neighborhood adored her. Whenever she took a stroll, they were sure of being treated to ice cream or chocolates.

Steve remonstrated with her mildly. He had always thought the French were a thrifty lot. She laughed. The French could spend money along with the best in the world, providing there was money to spend. Besides, she was certain that when the time came for her to be thrifty, she would clutch her francs as tightly as the next one.

"But," said Steve, "whenever I want to buy you a jewel or some other gift, you remind me that I shouldn't throw my money away."

"You give me sufficient," she replied gaily. "Besides, I have this emerald pendant which is worth a fortune."

All Steve could do was shrug, a Gallic habit he had mastered much better than French, which he still spoke abominably.

Steve was deeply concerned with Jacqueline's welfare. She meant more to him than he was willing to confess. Not that he admitted that he was in love with her; but she was becoming a habit, a pleasant and comfortable habit. There were so many facets to this girl. Girl? Yes, a mere girl who was proving to be more of a woman than any he had ever known. She was so easy to talk to. He had told her all of his intimate secrets. She knew every detail of his youth, his home in the Midwest. She was genuinely interested in everything he described. Even when he spoke of the

PTA, her absorption gave the commonplace an aura of glamor.

"Ah," she murmured when he replied to her inquiries regarding the function of the PTA. "Such wonder, so intelligent, how American!"

That is why a cable from his home office upset him. Ordinarily, it would have been routine; but now there was Jacqueline. He was required to spend some time in his London office. This meant separation, and he discovered he did not want to be separated from Jacqueline. He feared that she might refuse to leave Paris, and that upon his return, he might be unable to resume his wonderful relationship. He considered discussing the matter with Abelard, but immediately rejected this approach, for he had developed a guilt complex concerning the way Abelard had maneuvered Vishevsky into Jacqueline's bad graces.

After all, Vishevsky had poured his gratitude into the nude in Jacqueline's bathtub, all unsuspecting. Rumors had reached Steve that Vishevsky was drowning himself in vodka in some flea-ridden flat in St. Germain des Prés, refusing all commissions to paint bathtubs. He regretted his part in the Vishevsky affair. What he had not heard was that this actually was the best thing that could have happened to the artist. The unwashed Russian had turned back to the medium of canvas, attacking this material with such diligence that he was slowly but surely obtaining a minor importance as a true artist, not just an illustrator of nudes on bathroom fixtures.

Deciding against seeking Abelard's aid, Steve forthrightly informed Jacqueline that he had to leave for London within a few days. Either she would accompany him or not. Jacqueline replied that she would give him her answer on the following day when he returned from work. He sighed. He knew that she would ask the advice of her "board of advisers."

XXVIII

"THIS TIME of the year," the Duke pronounced, "Cannes, Nice, I can understand, even San Remo—but London!" He shuddered. "Why everybody who is anybody goes to the Riviera!"

Henri the Egg wiped the perspiration from his bare scalp, "Only we unfortunate working stiffs remain in Paris."

Flic ran his sleeve under his nose and muttered, "And tight-fisted tourists!"

The others seated in conference in La Tête nodded in unison.

Abelard ticked off, "Your friend DuMont has taken leave of the Chambre des Deputés to review our defenses at Antibes. That manufacturer of automobiles I introduced you to confers in Capri. Prince Igor. . ."

Jacqueline, seated demurely nearby, interrupted petulantly, "I asked for your thoughts regarding Steve's invitation to London, not for a roll call of my friends."

Abelard gesticulated authoritatively, "Patience, *chérie!* We must observe your problem from all degrees of the compass, weighing the advantages and the disadvantages. First, we must admit that because of the stifling weather, we appear to be the only ones left in Paris to keep you company."

Alsace's dolorous tones denied this. "Not the only ones. . ."

They gazed at him inquiringly. He pointed.

"Look what the hot wind has blown in."

Their heads jerked around. Vannois had just entered, accompanied by Suzanne. He nodded a greeting, then indicated a table near the "board of advisers" to Solan who was behind his bar.

"We'll sit there, bring a bottle of cognac."

Suzanne paused near Michel, "Say, next Sunday, how about you and a couple of your friends having a picnic at the *bois* with us girls?"

Michel appeared ill at ease. Abelard chuckled, "Since when are you angels permitted to spread your wings away from Au Paradis?"

Vannois bristled, "Madame, my wife, is a most kindly employer. The happiness of our girls comes first with her." He turned to Jacqueline. "She is most worried about you. Only this morning she said, 'Vannois, that pretty girl from the country, Jacqueline, I wish she would come and talk to me. There are rumors she may be heading into difficulties.' "

"The only difficulty Jacqueline has," assured the Duke, "is being considered by us—an invitation to travel abroad."

Suzanne's face lit up with envy. "Really? I'll bet with your American!"

Vannois shook his head disapprovingly, "Travel broadens difficulties. In a foreign country you may find yourself alone, with only strangers to turn to. If anything should happen ... " He shrugged, throwing up his hands, as though predicting the direst of all disasters.

"Hah!" It was Abelard seeing the light. "I must thank you, Vannois!"

Vannois was startled. He took a step back, his eyes becoming wary, as though he expected Abelard to produce a coiled viper.

Abelard slapped the table and chuckled. He turned to the others, "I knew deep in the pit of my stomach that there was something to bother me about this trip to London. Vannois has made it clear! The difficulty of being alone in a strange land!"

"But," protested Jacqueline, "I shall not be alone."

"Most of the day, you would be. Steve goes there for business. In London they are far more serious about business than here. While he is at business, you will be alone, *n'est-ce pas?*"

Jacqueline nodded.

"Therefore, being alone, you will suffer the ennui of loneliness."

"But to travel is an opportunity to obtain knowledge," Jacqueline replied.

"Hah!" Abelard's eyes rolled upward as though calling upon the gods to hear him. "Here is a woman of logic for you!" He appealed to his companions, "She has already made up her mind, and merely consults us as a salve to her conscience!"

"That is not so!" Jacqueline denied. "I have always relied on your experience to guide me; but I must admit a visit to a foreign city does intrigue me."

"And so it should, *ma petite,*" the Duke agreed. "Travel has its advantages. To accept Steve's invitation would not be a disaster."

Jacqueline nodded thoughtfully, and then stood up, *"Merci,* my friends, if I do go, it will only be for a few days."

"Well, then," concluded Abelard, "it's settled."

Jacqueline smiled, "I do not think it will be too lonely." She turned and called to Solan, "Solan, a carafe for my friends." She placed some currency on the table and left.

Tiny and Flic hitched their chairs closer to the table. Abelard smiled cavalierly at Suzanne.

"Join us, my pretty, and we will consider *your* invitation to the *bois*."

"How—how about me?" Vannois asked uncertainly.

"If," grumbled Tiny, "you spare me the *bon mots* of your witch of a wife, pull up a chair!"

With alacrity, Vannois pushed a chair to the edge of the group. Suzanne, who had been watching the departure of Jacqueline, turned with a look of frank admiration.

"Ah, that country girl! She has more the air of a virgin now than when I first saw her!"

Abelard leered, "And why not? In her conscience, she is still unwrapped!" His hand dropped to Suzanne's thigh and pressed. Suzanne tittered.

Solan brought the carafe of wine and scooped up the money Jacqueline had left. Abelard filled the glasses already on the table.

"We drink bon voyage to our girl, Solan."

"Ah," Solan inquired, "she has decided on London?"

Abelard nodded as he handed a glass of wine to Suzanne.

"Then," said Solan, "I must get busy. She will require a basket of food to endure the channel."

"Channel? What channel?" Abelard's brow furrowed.

Solan gave him a look of superiority, "The only one between here and that foggy land of tasteless beef and kidney pie!"

He marched toward the kitchen. The Duke hissed into Abelard's ear, "They go first class by air. They will require no basket of food!"

Abelard winked, "You know that. I know that. But Solan does not."

"Ah," the others chorused happily.

"For once," Abelard sniggered, "the bon voyage gift will comfort those who remain behind!"

The Duke raised his glass, "You are sometimes a greater rogue than I, my Abelard!" All agreed heartily.

Suddenly, Michel slammed his empty glass onto the table.

"Say, how do we know Solan'll permit Jacqueline to hand over the basket to us?"

Abelard eyed him pityingly. "Why I allow you to profit from my wisdom, I do not know. Solan cannot leave here with a business to attend. His basket of gustatory creations will be entrusted to us for delivery. And the day when Jacqueline is to leave, tomorrow, is Sunday."

"So?" shrugged Alsace. "And the next day is Monday."

Abelard sighed, "Where have you been? Have we not had an invitation to picnic in the *bois?*"

Michel exploded, *"Tolderolloll!* With Suzanne, Yvette, Roxanne . . . !"

"And myself. . . ."

Abelard's head shot around. Vannois grinned at him over his glass of wine.

"Yourself," Abelard agreed, "providing you supply an additional basket, and enough of companions to make a day in the woods worthwhile."

Before Vannois could reply, Suzanne spoke up.

"I agree. One basket and three girls will be insufficient to enjoy the woods. Also, perhaps during Jacqueline's absence, arrangements can be made concerning her empty apartment."

"Perhaps," Abelard grinned.

Vannois sipped his wine. He would have preferred cognac. This picnic! He would have to keep it secret from Madame Vannois. He shuddered in his mind. Her strident voice already filled his imagination.

"Drunkard! I send you to obtain evidence to eliminate Jacqueline, and you obtain for us these taxi clients who can afford only the cheapest of *vin du pays!*"

Aha, my stupid cabbage, Vannois smiled to himself, *I am boring from within! These idiot cab drivers will reveal all the evidence we require!*

He refilled his glass and laughed:

"Without a boast,
  I propose a toast!
  There is nothing more fair
  Than Bois du Boulogne air
  With wine for girls,
  And cognac for boys
  To savor life's little joys!"

"Why, Vannois," Suzanne marveled, "you improve in your poetry!"

She entwined herself around the preening little man, kissing him passionately. His eyes rolled, as though he had suddenly been enveloped by a bolt of lightning. The Duke winked at

Abelard and roared, "Vannois! At Au Paradis, I'll wager you were never this close to Paradise!"

Vannois paid no attention. He was enjoying Suzanne with more gusto than if she had been Napoleon brandy.

XXIX

ALREADY DUSK cast inky hues on the rippling waters of the Seine. Here and there, the city's lights reflected on its changing surface. It appeared to Jacqueline, gazing from the window of her apartment, that Paris was pulling the veil of night over its face to obscure the sadness of departure for a strange land.

She knew that she would merely be bidding the city of lights *"au revoir."* But, already that loneliness that Abelard had warned her about was seeping into her bones. Perhaps she would not have had this feeling if Steve had not been detained at his office. If this happened here, how much longer would be her lonely hours in London? She glanced back, suddenly becoming aware of Pierre's omnipresent eyes. For the first time she felt those orbs pierce her with utter disapproval. She strode from one end of the room to the other. Pierre's eyes followed her. She remembered how Abelard had cautioned her about the photograph. Impulsively, she shouted at it.

"Stop gazing at me as though you were a magistrate!" But, of course, Pierre paid her no heed.

"You must understand! Steve means nothing to me! It is *business!*"

Pierre gave no indication of understanding.

"*Stupide!*" she accused, and impulsively turned Pierre's face to the wall.

Her telephone jangled. She turned to it with a start. Undoubtedly it was Steve calling to apologize for being so late. She picked up the instrument.

"Allo, *chérie. . .*"

Prince Igor's voice murmured through to her.

"But," she stammered, "I thought you had departed for the Côte d'Azur!"

"No, no, no," he assured her. "At the last moment I

shuddered at the thought of going there with only that skeleton, Alec. Then I realized that you could really make the sun shine for me. Please be my guest."

"I regret," Jacqueline was contrite, "already there is a previous invitation."

"But not like mine," Igor assured her. "You have never seen the Blue Coast. I have not been there in ages. Together, we shall be like children discovering the sun for the first time."

Jacqueline's laughter tinkled. She did not see Steve let himself into the apartment.

"The waters of the Mediterranean," Igor persuaded, "are waiting to caress you with their warm fingers. . . ."

"Ah," Jacqueline teased, "such fingers will have to caress me another time. . . ."

Steve stood there, his ears virtually flapping.

"Then, at night, we will relax over the chessboard. I am always amused by the moves you make, defying all rules."

Jacqueline giggled, "Rules are made to be broken. But no matter how cleverly I move, you usually manage to pierce my defenses and leave me helpless!"

Righteously indignant, Steve strode over to her and snatched the phone from her hand. He slammed it down, cutting off Igor.

"How the hell can you carry on such intimate talk with another man!"

She stared at him as though he had suddenly lost his mind. "Intimate? Are you zigzag?"

"I haven't touched a drop! And I know what I heard!"

Jacqueline studied his face and then she gurgled knowingly, "Ah, the monster of green eyes upsets you!"

"All right, so I'm jealous! I've got a right to be!"

"One moment!" She raised a hand to silence him. "I do not care for this jealousy."

"Neither do I!" he assured her. "That's why I want you to go to London with me. Away from all this!" He encompassed the apartment with a circular motion.

"Please, Steve," she cautioned, "do not pretend a sentiment so emotional."

"What do I have to do? Turn caveman and hit you on the head? I'm in love with you! I want to marry you!"

Jacqueline studied him gravely, then shook her head. "To get married is not for us."

"Who's going to stop us? Pierre?" He jerked a thumb toward the photograph, without looking at it.

"*Non*. It is yourself."

"But I'm proposing!"

"What? That I shall accompany you to your home in the middle of America as your wife?"

He nodded.

"Consider then, as I preside over your home. I receive your so proper American wives. They speak to me. *Oui*, Madame, I say, I have been with Steve in Paris. But *certainement*, Paris is of a difference, without ladies' clubs like yours. The PTA? But of course I shall join. Perhaps even I shall be president. . . ."

Steve shuffled uneasily. He cleared his throat. "My love will make a real American out of you in no time."

"Ah, but I am French. I do not wish to desert La Belle France. Nor to accept a love which I know is a mistake. Between us, the agreement was of business, without the existence of emotion. I regret we must say adieu."

"But . . . but . . ." Steve sputtered, as Jacqueline headed away from him. His eye fell on the photograph, reversed to the wall.

"Why—why—is Pierre facing the wall?" he demanded.

"That," replied Jacqueline, "is my business."

She picked up the telephone and dialed.

"Igor," she said, "I wish to accept your invitation, if you will have me." She listened. "Of course I can be ready in the morning."

She hung up and gazed at Steve, who was a study in utter misery. She went over to him and took his hand.

"Chéri, already Pierre stares at the wall. Why waste it?"

He grabbed her, kissing her feverishly. Startled by his uncommon ardor, she backed away, tripping. They fell against the bed which knocked into the wall.

The thump caused the picture to shake and slowly wind around on its wire.

"Oh, no!" Steve protested.

Pierre's face dangled from the wire, glaring directly into Steve's widening eyes.

Jacqueline looked up and sighed.

"Ah, Pierre, Pierre! Must you add to the difficulties of my collecting a dowry!"

XXX

A BRISK wind blew from the Seine, rippling through the leafy crowns of the city's stately trees. A benign sun warmed the countless patrons of the sidewalk cafés. Pedestrians overflowed the boulevards as they promenaded gaily.

It was a day which clothed the beautiful metropolis with that brilliance which has always dazzled the world, renewing old loves, kindling new ones, making visitors gasp as though they had suddenly come upon unexpected giant canvases of the most inspired of Old Masters.

The dome of Les Invalides shone brilliantly. The old stones of Notre Dame reflected brilliantly. The waters of the Seine sparkled brilliantly. The cerulean heavens were alight brilliantly. Everywhere the sun poked its heavenly rays brilliantly. Everywhere, except La Tête. Oh, to be sure, sunlight smiled in the vicinity of the café, even casting its warmth within. But in the hearts of the café's "regulars" no sun could penetrate. There they sat, huddled about a table, diffidently toying with coffee or wine. Several bluebottle flies buzzed and zoomed without once being cursed or slapped at. Solan sat behind his bar, idly riffling the pages of a magazine, his face long and gloomy. There was a sameness of gloom in all of them—Abelard, the Duke, Henri the Egg, Alsace, Michel, Tiny and Flic. At a nearby table, Vannois stared fixedly at an untouched glass of cognac, paying little attention to Suzanne, Yvette and Roxanne who appeared to be on the verge of tears. The only sound came deep from the throats of the taxi drivers, as one or the other sighed heavily. Vannois took a sip of his drink and then, apparently finding it unenjoyable, pushed it away from him and stood up.

"Well," he said resignedly, "since there is no solution, I suppose we might as well return to Au Paradis."

"Return to Au Paradis?" Suzanne was unenthusiastic. "For what? To be a barmaid? There isn't enough business for *half* a barmaid!"

"At least there is a roof remaining over your heads." He

128

glanced at the taxi drivers, "I never thought there would be a time when you could not solve a problem."

Abelard snorted, "If it weren't for the girls, I'd let you stew in your wife's juices!"

Vannois laughed bitterly, "That would be a stew as dry as the Sahara. Madame is already shriveling like a mummy over this situation."

The Duke spat out, "She deserves such desiccation! If she had not been so vengeful, she would have been allowed to remain obscure—and in business!"

"Hear! Hear!" the others approved.

"But," protested Roxanne, "we, too, have no business, in addition to no money!"

A pall of deeper gloom settled over the café. At this sad moment, a glorious being happily appeared in the doorway. The bright sunshine cast its halo around her form, her auburn hair reflected like living flame.

"*Hola! Mes amis!* I have returned!"

It was a moment electric—a tableau of stunned silence, of incredulity, of men staring at an apparition of hope and beauty, not one daring to make any movement that would destroy this charming mirage.

"Jacqueline!" Abelard exploded with delight, and cannon-aded toward her.

"Jacqueline!"

Solan and the others were a bombardment of welcome as they crowded around their prodigal. Laughing happily, she embraced first one, then the other, until she came on Vannois, who was shifting uneasily from one foot to the other.

"Even you," she declared, "I am delighted to see!"

She kissed his cheek.

Abelard grumbled, "In a moment, you will want him hanged, drawn and quartered."

Jacqueline darted a glance at Abelard, reacting to his glowering expression. Her eyes flitted to the others. Gloomily, they all nodded.

"Him and his wife," Tiny rumbled. "They tried to put you out of business."

"Tried? Hah!" the Duke snorted. "Only too well have they succeeded! Not only have they put you out of business, but also Suzanne, Roxanne, Yvette, and themselves!"

"But—but—how is that possible?" Jacqueline was bewildered.

Flic wiped his nose, "The law of Marie Richard."

"But," said Jacqueline, "this law has always been impractical."

"Of course," Abelard nodded, "for thousands of years such laws have been impractical; but for the time being it is being enforced. And it is all the fault of Madame Vannois."

"Who," added Suzanne acidly, "places all the blame on you."

"I? I wouldn't know such a law if it bit me!" Jacqueline retorted.

The Duke nodded, "It's a devious tale, and can be best told by that sniffer of cognac!" His finger leveled accusingly at Vannois.

Vannois shifted as though seeking escape. Tiny collared him and plumped him down on a chair. Vannois sighed.

"What could I do? Madame has me under her domination. She orders, I obey."

Steely eyes met his pleading ones. He wilted, running his tongue over his drying lips. He nervously picked up a glass of wine and gulped it down.

"Speak up!" Abelard commanded.

Vannois' voice was apologetic. "Madame felt that you were bringing anarchy to places like Au Paradis," he looked at Jacqueline. "She felt if the proper attention were brought to you, certain quarters would be compelled to cast you out."

"Put her in jail, you mean!" Alsace accused.

Vannois shrugged helplessly, "Madame was prepared to keep you out of the Bastille by giving you employment in our licensed café."

"Haw!" Abelard snorted. "Lot of good her license does now!"

"Somehow, attention was brought to certain establishments whose discreet operation was unofficially protected by . . ."

"Somehow, *merde!*" Suzanne picked up the story. "Just before you left for the Mediterranean with your Prince, Madame tipped off a newspaperman that awful things were happening here and in your apartment. He fell in on us while we, that is, us girls, and our good friends, these honest, hard-working taxi drivers, prepared to have a picnic. Well, how were we to know that he would invite himself along as a spy!"

Roxanne nodded emphatically, "We selected a most out-of-the-way place in the *bois*. The thick bushes gave us the privacy of a boudoir. But not from that stinking sneak's camera!"

"He took pictures of *everything!*" Yvette moaned.

Michel nodded sheepishly, "There was an especially active one of me . . . with Suzanne."

The Duke grinned, "Of all of us. He was most thorough, much to everyone's misfortune. He obtained our identities and cooperated with the police after the accident."

"What accident?" Jacqueline was fascinated.

"Well," explained the Duke, "the accident at the Arc de Triomphe which tied up traffic for several hours. You see, there was more than sufficient wine at the picnic—"

"Which we drank," came Alsace's dolorous tones, "becoming very drunk."

"A condition," Henri the Egg shook his baldness sadly, "which caused us to steer our taxis merrily in all directions."

"In our alcoholic happiness," said Suzanne, "we belonged to Paris and Paris belonged to us. Unfortunately, the policemen disagreed with this ownership, so," she shrugged, "I bit one on the nose."

"I," said Roxanne, "hit another on the head with my shoe."

"The other four," rumbled Tiny, "we rendered *hors de combat.*"

"All of which," Abelard concluded, "was duly recorded for posterity by the journalist's camera, causing us to pay tremendous fines. Hardly had we been released from behind iron bars, when unhappy police egged on by irate women's organizations swooped down on Au Paradis depriving these girls of home and livelihood."

"Surely," said Yvette, "you read about this in the papers last week."

Jacqueline shook her head, "I was too busy playing—ah—chess."

The Duke sighed, "In time, this will be like the dust of history, and conditions will permit us to play—ah—chess, as you call it. At the moment, vengeful organizations of wives shriek out their morality to prevent husbands and bachelors from being normal happy beings." He shrugged energetically, indicating that the situation could extend into infinity.

"Fortunately," Abelard concluded, "the visit of the police to La Tête and your apartment confounded Madame Vannois' charges. Your friends, most prominently your American, assured them that you are associated in the sale of art and Solan is a chef of renown."

"Steve has returned from London?"

Abelard nodded, "He was gone only two days. He drops by every day."

Jacqueline remained thoughtful for a moment. "Well, I suppose if he desires, we can continue with his French lessons." Suddenly a brightness filled her face, "That may be a solution!"

There was a silence, a dead silence interrupted only by Flic's sniffling. Abelard sipped some wine.

"For you, yes," he said slowly. "But we cannot suddenly make language teachers of these three." He indicated the other girls. "We may, perhaps, discover careers more suitable for them."

Solan made a suggestion, "Here at La Tête, who can say how many girls I may employ, without salaries, of course."

"Too undignified," the Duke waved him aside. "I feel Jacqueline's suggestion, however, can be elaborated properly. With so great a tourist trade in Paris, a tutoring service cannot be questioned.".

"Ha!" Abelard's eyes sparkled. "Provided it were linked to a service of guides to the more interesting sections of the city!"

Vannois put forth timorously, "This business, could the offices be at Au Paradis?"

The eyes of the cab drivers speared him. Abelard looked down his nose at the little man.

"This is a business of individuals who will have signs describing the discreet services offered and their qualifications, which do not include a padlocked place."

"Hey," exclaimed Michel, "we could carry such signs in our taxis!"

"Precisely," nodded Abelard.

Suzanne stretched herself to her full queenly height and haughtily gestured.

"Run along, Vannois. Inform Madame that our arrangement has come to its end."

"One moment," Jacqueline remarked. "Since Au Paradis, itself, is out of business, it appears a shame that we cannot make use of it." Vannois looked hopeful. "With the proper remodeling, why can it not be redesigned for a comfortable headquarters for the most attractive guided tours in Paris?"

The Duke laughed, "You have it, *ma fille!*" He turned to Vannois, "If Madame can be made to see the light, she may obtain certain rents, no more."

Gloom was dissipated. Bright sunlight poured through the passing clouds, cheerily and delightfully.

"A toast," Suzanne called out, "a toast to Jacqueline!"

Solan hurried over with wine and glasses. Abelard and Tiny lifted Jacqueline to a table and all gathered around to drink to her, even Vannois.

"At last, you're back!"

Abelard whirled about, shouting, "Steve! Welcome! Welcome! You are in time to celebrate a recovery from our disaster because of Jacqueline's intelligence!"

Jacqueline looked down gravely at Steve. He jumped up on the table beside her and kissed her. She accepted his lips calmly.

"I accept your kiss, as a friend, Steve, but nothing more."

A silence struck the others. Steve appeared sheepish, but he was determined to have his say.

"I know a lost cause when I butt my head against it, Jacqueline, but I owe you a good deal."

"You owe me nothing, Steve," she replied softly.

"Stop me if I'm wrong. You came to Paris to earn a dowry, so you could return home, marry Pierre, and live happily ever after." Steve paused. She said nothing. "Once you collect your dowry, there's nothing to keep you here, isn't that so?"

She nodded.

"I proposed to you. Unfortunately, you don't love me. But I still want you to have what you *want*. Your Pierre, your farm, your dowry. You've got the first two." He took some papers from his pocket and handed them to her. "Here's the third. Title to your beautiful machine."

Jacqueline offered the papers back, "I cannot accept. I haven't paid for it."

"Sweetheart," Steve insisted, "Earth-King is having a white elephant close-out sale, and we've closed out that machine for the amount you've already paid in. The machine is yours, all yours!"

He jumped off the table.

"I hope you and Pierre will live happily for the next hundred years."

Before Jacqueline could reply, Steve turned and strode out. She stared wistfully after him.

"Hey," said Abelard, "the hell with this." He slammed his glass of wine on the floor. "I don't like saying goodbyes!"

Tears welled in Jacqueline's eyes. Her lips trembled. There was such a heavy lump of sadness within her that she felt leaden. Why it was so, she could not understand. The machine, the machine was hers, and she could return triumphant to Pierre. She should be dancing and laughing; but she had no desire to do so.

Abelard, the Duke, the others shimmered before her as she dabbed at her eyes.

"I, too," she said, "am most unhappy to say goodbye." She slid down from the table.

XXXI

PIERRE CLIMBED over the small stone wall that separated his farm from that of Yvonne, the recently bereaved daughter of farmer Bouchard, whose heart had failed him during an argument over the price of lamb with the local butcher. Pierre glanced about the land adjoining his. It was much larger. Combined with his farm, it would be one of the most prosperous in the province. Upon old Bouchard's departure from this earthly sphere, it was only natural for Pierre to offer his well-muscled shoulder and arms to the desolated Yvonne. She accepted his solace with alacrity. A marriage between them, Pierre considered, would be more than neighborly. It would be most wise. She would bring him a farm, an entire farm, as a dowry. Of course she was not as well formed, nor desirable as Jacqueline, but she was a workhorse. A farmer needed a worker far more than he required beauty.

And land. There was nothing better than land. Of course he could not marry Yvonne at once. First, there should be a proper interval between the burial of her father and the dancing at a wedding. Secondly, he was a man of honor. He simply couldn't break his vow of betrothal to Jacqueline. However, if she could be made to understand in some subtle manner that her future lay with another man, then he would gracefully release her.

The rumbling of a powerful engine distracted him. He raised a hand to shade his eyes from the glare of the sun. In the distance, approaching his farm, a huge, monstrous vehicle, a truck bearing a canvas-covered object, churned through the dust of the road. He wondered what such a vehicle was doing here. Undoubtedly a driver who had lost his way. He walked toward it. The noise of the truck echoed over the land. A shrill voice called to him. He looked back. Yvonne came running toward him from her farmhouse, as fast as her stubby legs could carry her. She easily climbed the stone wall, and hurried over to him. Her small eyes peered toward the vehicle.

"What is it?"

Pierre shrugged, "Undoubtedly a confused truck driver."

They stood in the middle of the road as the truck sped toward them. In a few minutes it stopped.

"Jacqueline!" Pierre's jaw dropped open as his fiancée, quickly stepped out of the cab and ran to him. She halted abruptly as she noticed Yvonne standing close to Pierre. Yvonne's hand snaked out and grasped Pierre's. This was not a sight Jacqueline had expected. There they stood, two peasants, seeming to present a united front against an invader from the city. They seemed to belong together. Jacqueline tossed her head as though to chase this thought away.

"I am back, Pierre," she said simply. Her eyes took in all of Pierre swiftly. He seemed so dirty. A stranger almost.

"You are back," Pierre affirmed dully. "You have come back, and it isn't a year."

Jacqueline laughed, "I told you when I came back, I would bring the greatest dowry ever seen. *Voilà!*"

She waved at the truck. The driver already was untying the canvas cover.

"What is it?" asked Yvonne. She and Pierre moved closer to Jacqueline. Jacqueline sniffed. How they smelled! Like a barn filled with manure! She took Pierre's arm despite the wave of distaste that swept through her. Could it be possible that in such a short time she had grown away from this farmland? She tossed her head slightly and smiled.

"It is a machine, a wonderful, magnificent, formidable machine! There is no farmer I know who can afford such a machine!"

The driver uncovered the machine. Pierre gasped.

"Truly, no farmer could afford such a machine!"

Yvonne sniffed, "If he could, he wouldn't be able to use it. It is too much of a machine."

Pierre shook loose from Jacqueline. He walked this way, then that way, studying the machine.

"It is a stupid machine," he decided, "much too stupid for use on any farm around here. Why this is not a machine to plant and harvest a farm. It is a machine that could gulp up a whole province, a nation! It would not be suitable on my land!"

"Why not?" asked Jacqueline. "In the instructions it explains that this machine, when properly handled, will suit any farm."

"Don't tell me my business," declared Pierre. "My farm requires no such machine. It is a ridiculous dowry. The money invested in it is a total loss. It takes up a great amount of space and I am short of space."

As he spoke, Yvonne kept nodding emphatically, inching in closer to Pierre.

"My father, rest in peace, would agree with you, Pierre."

"Oh," said Jacqueline sympathetically, "I had not heard. My sympathy on your bereavement."

"I accept it," Yvonne said flatly, then simpered, "If it were not for Pierre, I would never have been able to bear up under it."

Pierre was abashed. "Naturally, since we are neighbors ... you know how it is...." He put his arm around Yvonne's shoulder.

"Of course," said Jacqueline, feeling her heart lighten, "I now how it is." She looked directly at Yvonne, "And, naturally you have a ready-made dowry, your farm, which any young man would be happy with."

"Not *any* young man," she said archly.

"And," she turned to Pierre, "my machine is not so wonderful to you in comparison to additional land."

"I didn't say that," Pierre grumbled defensively. "It is just that a simple farmer could not afford to own such a machine. However, as we are betrothed, and you have it as your dowry, I might overlook such a mistake and ... "

Jacqueline laughed and raised a hand as if in benediction, "Bless you, my children, and may you have many, many little farms and farmers. I—I go back to Paris where I now realize I belong."

She turned away before Pierre could say anything and called out, "Georges, we have come to the wrong place. The machine is to be delivered to the village."

She ran quickly to the truck and got into the cab. Georges covered the machine, got behind the wheel and, not caring a fig for anything fore and aft of the huge truck, backed around and sped toward Jacqueline's natal village.

XXXII

THE MACHINE occupied the center of the village. It loomed massively in the square, its brightness giving the drab surroundings the brilliance of carnival. It stood there, a colossus of steel, fiercesome and awesome, casting a nightmare of shadows over the few shops and homes of the town. Children and grownups stared, some in disbelief, others in admiration. Curiosity drew them from the shops. The daily routine of business was at a standstill. The baker's delivery boy ignored the fresh loaves of bread jutting from the basket of his three-wheeled cycle. The butcher and his wife stood in the entrance of their *boucherie*, arms folded across their stout bellies, conjecturing on the meaning of this mountainous presence. Then, forthrightly, someone touched and felt the strength in this machine, venturing that it was sent by the government to tear up the roads as a preliminary to widening them. Another disagreed, it could, perhaps, be a new type of military weapon. A small boy with ragged trousers jumped up into the seat, happily screeching, "I'm a spaceman! Look at me fly!" Immediately, his mother dragged him down and shook him.

"Aw," he said, "it don't scare me! There was a girl who brought it. She's in there!"

He pointed a dirt-encrusted hand toward the mayor's home. As if this were a signal, the mayor, resplendent in his official hat and chain of office, came out with Jacqueline.

"Ah," he declared, "it is, indeed, formidable!"

The villagers streamed toward him.

"*Mes amis,*" the mayor began pompously, "on this day

one of our daughters has returned with a gift unheard of for our beautiful village."

"Why," someone declared, "it's Jacqueline!"

"Hey," a man shouted good-naturedly, "what sort of gift do you bring us!"

Another man called out with equal good humor, "It's enough you bring yourself back. You're something to look at!"

Jacqueline burst into laughter. It was epidemic. Everybody laughed. Jacqueline called out.

"Myself you haven't seen every day like your own women, so I look good. In a week, two weeks, you'll notice me less than a good leg of mutton!"

The crowd renewed its laughter. The mayor held up his hands for silence.

"*Mes amis,* never in the history of our fair village has such a gift been delivered. A machine for everyone, at a cost to no one, which can work the land, harvest a crop, plant the seed. It will give us time from our hard labor to enjoy more of our leisure."

A cheer went up, "Bravo, Jacqueline!"

The mayor beamed, then took Jacqueline by the arm and escorted her to the machine. "I have a proposal," he announced. "In honor of our generous citizeness I, personally, will provide a bottle of champagne to dedicate this machine which shall forever be called 'Jacqueline.' "

"That," replied Jacqueline, "is an honor I do not require."

"She's right!" Old Thibault, the owner of the town's car-for-hire, pushed his way to the fore, "Let us remember it as the machine of Jacqueline and drink the champagne!"

A roar of approval met this suggestion.

"But," protested the mayor nervously, "one bottle of champagne would hardly be enough."

"Then," said Old Thibault, "dip into the treasury and let's have a party!"

"Oh, my," said the mayor, unable to stem the tide of people who suddenly marched toward the town's lone tavern, which was owned by him.

"Oh, I am sorry," Jacqueline apologized contritely, "I did not intend for this to happen."

The mayor sighed, "It is nothing. They will not drink much. Besides, it will be of good service, this party, to keep me longer in office." He turned and sighed again as he viewed the machine, "It is a wonderful machine, but it would be much more wonderful if it were a new school."

"A new school?" Jacqueline could not see the connection.

The mayor nodded, "It is not that I do not appreciate the sentiment and unselfishness of this gift, nor that we shall not be able to put it to good use; but for years, I have been dreaming and hoping that our village should have a new school, with broad and airy windows. Each year I have sent a request to the government and each year the same form letter returns in reply. Our old school must be surveyed. But no one ever comes to survey."

"A new school?" Jacqueline's question was an expression of her thinking. "And how much would a new school cost?"

"Oh," replied the mayor, "I really have no idea. But I should judge it would cost five, perhaps ten times as much as this machine you have so generously donated to us."

"Oh, as much as that?" Jacqueline became lost in thought, then murmured as if to herself, "That would take more than a year."

"Heh? What's that?" asked the mayor.

"It is very important, a new school?"

The mayor nodded soberly, "We are much crowded in the old school, and many find it difficult to reach. A new school would be placed where all could come to it, from all over this district. There would be an appeal for education then, and of all things for our children, education is the finest."

"Hmm!" Jacqueline considered. "It is a tremendous amount of money, but it can be managed. However, if you do not mind waiting two or three years, you shall have your school."

"Wait two or three years! Why," the astonished mayor declared, "I have been waiting ten years, two or three would be as nothing!"

"It is settled, then!" Jacqueline assured him. "I return to Paris where I shall devote myself to buying you this new school!"

The mayor stared in disbelief. His eyes swiveled from Jacqueline to the machine and back again. Awe and gratefulness filled his face.

"Ordinarily, if a young girl, no matter how generous and beautiful, should say such a thing, I would call for our doctor. But when I see you, and then I see this machine, I know this is not ordinarily! But—so much money—it—it seems impossible!"

"With the connections I have made in so many important and high places, I know it will not be impossible. I shall build you this school!"

"Bless you! Bless you!" The mayor took off his chain of office and draped it around Jacqueline's neck. He kissed both her cheeks and then offered her his arm. "You must be my guest in my tavern!"

"Ordinarily, I should be most happy to accompany you," said Jacqueline soberly, "but every moment is golden now, and the driver and the truck must return to Paris at once, and I shall return with him."

"Then," said the mayor, "the whole town must be here to bid you *au revoir*."

He dashed for the tavern. Jacqueline walked along the street to where Georges and the truck were waiting. She stopped and looked back at the machine. The machine seemed to look back at her. Ah, it was such a thing of strength and beauty—and of a dream that she had possessed. She was happy in her heart that it would remain here in her own small village.

The mayor and the townspeople burst from the tavern and soon surrounded Jacqueline with shouts of fond farewell. A couple of the men lifted her bodily into the cab. Another heaped a few bottles of champagne onto her lap. There were many shouts of familiarity and love, chief of which was the mayor's "Forever you shall be at home in our hearts, Jacqueline!"

"Au revoir! Au revoir!"

The tremendous truck engine started. Jacqueline leaned out of the window and called out over its noise.

"I go to Paris! But I shall return, in two, perhaps three years!"

She waved at everyone. Everyone waved back. The mayor blew her a kiss, wiped his eyes, and blew his nose. The truck picked up speed, sending up a shower of dust beneath its heavy wheels. Georges shifted and the truck sped on at a steady rate. Jacqueline dabbed at her eyes.

"What are you crying for?" Georges inquired softly. "You are going to Paris where you belong."

Jacqueline nodded, "A moment of sentiment; but only a moment."

She settled back and picked up a bottle, "A good year,

Georges, you will join me and my friends at La Tête when we return."

Georges grinned, "Try and keep me away."

He began to whistle. Jacqueline craned her head to look back. A nice town, a nice village. But then, not for her. In her heart, her blood, there could only be one place—Paris.

She settled back comfortably. Ah, how surprised would they all be at La Tête! How pleased would her board of advisers be when they heard of her plans to purchase a school. The steady beat of the engine and the drone of the tires were like a lullaby. She relaxed and closed her eyes.

Jacqueline was going home.

THE END
of an Original Gold Medal Novel by
Nathaniel Tanchuck

ANOTHER IN THE BESTSELLING TRAVIS McGEE
SUSPENSE SERIES BY

John D. MacDonald

"John D. MacDonald keeps one reading with
fierce interest."

—N. Y. Herald Tribune Book Review

THE QUICK
RED FOX

From all that Travis McGee could gather
it must have been one hell of a party. Ten
playful people swinging wild and free, getting
drunk, getting bored, swapping partners in
the warmth of sun on naked bodies, miles
from civilization.

Miles from civilization—and 300 feet from
a very good camera with a telephoto lens.
The whole sordid show was down on film, and
the star attraction was a woman named Lysa
Dean whose professional life depended on her
private reputation.

It was a blackmail set-up as old as the hills
and Lysa was old enough to have known better. McGee didn't want to touch the deal
with a ten-foot pole—except there was another woman involved, a lovely, longing,
tender woman whose life was slowly draining
away into disaster. . . .

ON SALE NOW—ONLY 40¢

WHEREVER PAPERBACK BOOKS ARE SOLD

FAWCETT WORLD LIBRARY

K1464